LAND or DEATH

The Peasant Struggle in Peru

by Hugo Blanco

PATHFINDER PRESS, NEW YORK, 1972

Dedication

To my mother, who is suffering so much, with the promise that we will create a world of love.

To my comrades around the world, builders of the world party of the socialist revolution.

To heroic Indochina, vanguard of humanity.

Manufactured in the United States of America
Library of Congress Catalog Card Number 73-186689

First Edition, 1972

Translated by Naomi Allen

Pathfinder Press
410 West Street
New York, N. Y. 10014

Contents

Part I

Introduction by Peter Camejo ... 7

1 **The Sequence of Events** ... 19

2 **The Geographical, Economic and Social Setting** ... 25

3 **The Party** ... 36

4 **Two Lines** ... 41

5 **Dual Power** ... 53

6 **The Question of Armed Struggle and Putschism** ... 62

7 **Our Trial** ... 76

8 **Some Questions Answered** ... 83

Part II

Introductory Remarks ... 93

Open Letter to the Supreme Court of Military Justice ... 96

To My People ... 97

To the Congress of the Peruvian Federation of Students ... 98

Letter to Those Who Protested the Death Sentence ... 100

Puno ... 101

Puna, a story ... 103

Letter to a Peasant Leader ... 110

Simon Oviedo ... 116

Students: To the Countryside!   118

The Peasant Movement   120

The Teacher, a Story   126

My Tayta Jose Maria and the Indian Aspect
of the Peruvian Revolution   130

Peasant Work in the City   135

Free Vincente Lanado!   136

The Earthquake: The Rich and the Poor   139

The Government, the Oligarchy and the Exploited   145

To the Peasants of La Convencion and Lares   156

Notes   159

Glossary of Foreign Words   169

Index   173

Part I

Part I

Introduction

In recent years, the Quechua peasants have pressed forward in successive upsurges, seeking to reverse their intolerable position at the bottom of Peru's social structure. Their rebellion, coupled with that of the urban workers, threatens to topple the rule of the country's privileged upper classes and the foreign corporations that stand behind them. In this dynamic revolutionary process, the oppressed layers have found in Hugo Blanco a truly representative figure.

In his book *Cuzco: Tierra y Muerte,* the Peruvian journalist Hugo Neyra describes a mass meeting of peasants:

> In the Plaza de Armas in Cuzco the evening came, dressed in flaming red. The meeting of the peasants was languishing. The crowd, disciplined, standing, listened, applauded, laughed or yawned.
>
> Then a student came forward. It could have been Valer or Fausto Cornejo. He took the mike and shouted in Quechua: "Causachu Compañero Cuna, Hugo Blanco. . . ."
>
> The crowd awoke and responded with great shouts: "Causachu, Causachu, Causachu." [Viva! Viva! Viva!]
>
> I saw this repeated throughout the South. No other name arouses greater fervor among the men in striped ponchos who speak the euphonious Quechua. The shadow of Hugo Blanco was present at all the interviews I conducted in the South. I am not exaggerating: the unity of this agrarian movement that has no limits, like an immense ocean, whether in ideology or comportment, which can just as well turn peaceful and cooperative as explode in blood and gunfire, has, nevertheless, a name that unites the people of the mountains and the valleys, of the hacienda and the community — Hugo Blanco. . . .

There is nothing artificial about this feeling for Hugo Blanco. The reasons for it are rooted in the tempestuous history of the region.

While the first satellites circled the earth and jet airliners

landed in Lima, the Quechuas were still working the fields
of rich landlords without pay, like the serfs of medieval Europe. Peruvian peasants suffer a triple oppression: they are
oppressed as Peruvians by U. S. imperialism; as Quechuas
by Spanish-speaking whites and mestizos; and as workers
or peasants by capitalists and landowners. Peasant women
suffer, in addition, the oppression meted out to their sex under
capitalism, an oppression that is particularly harsh and ir-
rational in Latin America.

In the early sixties, this mass of one of the most oppressed
peoples in the Western Hemisphere began to rise. Tens of thousands did the unthinkable: they took back the lands stolen
from them, declared themselves human beings, stopped working for their exploiters, and began working for themselves.
In the vanguard of this struggle, which was also a struggle
to establish a new leadership, the most courageous and dar-
ing peasant unions arose in Chaupimayo.

Chaupimayo was the example, the inspiration. The lessons of
Chaupimayo, written with the sweat and blood of hundreds
of thousands of peasants, portrays for us the broad outlines
of Peru's future liberation.

By good fortune, the leader of Chaupimayo, Hugo Blanco,
still lives. And it is his own modest but clear and impressively
reasoned account of what happened and why that makes this
book unique. *Land or Death* describes how the peasantry
organized and made its own land reform. It explains how
the masses became convinced of the necessity for armed
struggle. Blanco takes every opportunity to indicate the limitations of the movement he led; he carefully points out what
was lacking to transform the powerful liberation struggle in
Chaupimayo into a nationwide revolution.

Of the books written in Latin America in the past decade
that seek to present a revolutionary strategy, none approaches
Blanco's in value. It is unique in three respects:

First, Blanco's conclusions are based on the actual experience of leading masses in struggle. All the other strategists
speak of the need to win the masses. Blanco has done it.

Second, it is now fashionable to criticize the concepts asso-
ciated with Régis Debray, above all the *foco* theory. Many,
like Héctor Béjar and Douglas Bravo, the two well-known
guerrilla leaders of Peru and Venezuela, respectively, now de-
plore their own underestimation of mass work and their
Debrayist errors. (Even Debray now criticizes Debrayism.)
But Blanco opposed Debrayism and *focoism* when it was
first advocated as a revolutionary strategy; he did so not

only in words but in action. Blanco led armed struggles that stemmed from mass movements, not from small groups of dedicated and courageous but, in the end, isolated men and women.

Third, Blanco clearly states what should be done. The others tend to question the past, to explain their errors, and to suggest possible solutions. *Land or Death* insists on what not to do, but more important, on what should be done.

Guerrillaism arose as a challenge to the reformist currents in Latin America. But it was an incomplete response. Although it correctly recognized the necessity of armed struggle, it left out the necessity of winning the masses politically. Thus, the two alternatives existing throughout the sixties for the left in Latin America were the opportunism of the Communist Party and other groups or separation from mass struggles through ultraleft armed actions. Both were dead ends. The guerrilla challenge to reformism in Latin America has, at the end of ten years, actually reinforced reformism.

This process is most clearly revealed by the support to the reformist, capitalist regimes in Chile and Peru from guerrilla currents that once swore undying opposition to capitalism and reformism. Some of the guerrillas are toying with the idea that perhaps, after all, a "peaceful road to socialism" may be found in certain exceptional countries, under certain exceptional circumstances. A consequence has been a resurgence of popular frontism in certain Latin American countries, such as Chile and Uruguay, and a decline in the number of advocates and practitioners of guerrilla war as a short-cut to power.

The experience in Chaupimayo shows that there is a third alternative. It is possible to develop a revolutionary strategy and to develop a mass base. The example of Chaupimayo is the answer to the current tendency of the left in Latin America to oscillate between mass work with a reformist program and seemingly revolutionary but isolated action. *Land or Death* explains how, through transitional steps, it is possible to convert a revolutionary program into mass revolutionary actions.

Because of this, *Land or Death*, in its modest way, constitutes one of the most significant contributions to the theory and practice of the Latin American revolution since the Cuban Revolution.

Blanco polemicizes dispassionately. He recognizes the self-sacrifice, honesty, and dedication of many of those with whom he disagrees. At the same time, he documents the betrayal of the peasants by those currents — primarily the Communist parties — that try to pass themselves off as revolutionary.

Blanco makes no pretensions. He points out the weakness of his own organization, the Frente de Izquierda Revolutionario (FIR — Revolutionary Left Front). He seeks to influence the reader by recounting and explaining the reality he lived, without glossing over the shortcomings or errors.

His message is profoundly proletarian and revolutionary: the workers and peasants must liberate themselves; the vanguard must learn how to avoid reformism and ultraleftism; they must learn how to reach the masses at their present level of consciousness and, by means of transitional measures, move them in action to a higher consciousness. Without a revolutionary party, this process will stagnate, unable to become generalized into a struggle for power.

Land or Death sums up twenty years of Hugo Blanco's political development as student, worker, and peasant. Born in Cuzco of a middle-class mestizo family, Blanco grew up fully aware of the superexploitation of the Quechuas. His father was a lawyer who handled cases for them. Blanco, as a child, heard stories at home of the injustices committed by the *gamonales* [bosses]. He heard firsthand accounts from the victims. He saw the courts ruling always in favor of the big landowners.

It is not surprising that the first conscious expression of his radicalization was a commitment to *Indianismo* — a tradition among radicalized intellectuals in Peru which can be summarized as the belief that Indians are human beings and should be treated as such — a rather dangerous concept in Peru.

As a youth Blanco became proud of his descent. Because he longed to know the history of his own people, the Incas, he was attracted to archaeology. He spent long days living among the Quechuas, learning their songs and becoming part of the Quechua world. His family gave him the opportunity to study. In 1954, still not twenty years old but already experienced in student struggles and illegal political work, Hugo Blanco traveled to Buenos Aires to study agronomy at the university.

There his early rebel inclinations matured. He rejected the opportunism of APRA (Alianza Popular Revolucionaria Americana) and the Communist Party, and joined the Trotskyist movement in Buenos Aires. He got his first trade-union experience there working in a meat-packing plant.

Soon after returning to Lima, Blanco found himself in danger of arrest because of his part in organizing the famous "reception" for then-vice-president Richard M. Nixon. The small Trotskyist group in Lima decided in the situation that followed that it would be best for Blanco to return to his native Cuzco.

Land or Death describes the events that led to his involvement in the peasant struggles in La Convención and Lares provinces near Cuzco.

It is a near miracle, owing in great part to his enormous popularity, that Hugo Blanco is alive today. Not only were there attempts to assassinate him before his capture in 1963, but the government sought to execute him "legally."

The police assigned to capture Hugo Blanco were under orders to shoot him on sight. Surprised, and surrounded in a small peasant hut, Blanco attempted to hide by flattening out in a mud wallow. The military search party consisted of troops who are especially hostile to peasants and some members of the Peruvian Political Police (PIP), one of whom discovered Blanco hiding in the mud.

He called out, "I've found him."

The head of the search party, a *Guardia Civil* officer, shouted back, "Shoot him!"

The PIP officer deliberately fired to one side, missing Blanco, but giving the impression that he had killed him. In the seconds before the rest of the troops arrived on the scene, he allowed Blanco to stand up, surrender, and be disarmed.

The returning *Guardia Civil* officer was furious. But he hesitated to assassinate the prisoner before so many witnesses, including the PIP officer who had refused to kill him. A similar incident saved Fidel Castro from assassination when he was captured after the Moncada Barracks raid of July 26, 1953.

After his capture, Blanco discovered that the PIP officer's reluctance to kill him had its counterpart in the sympathy shown him by many of the rank-and-file police and soldiers detailed to guard him. It is from the sons of the Peruvian poor that these repressive bodies recruit their rank-and-filers.

After his capture, he was marched barefoot to the nearest town, bleeding from a head wound inflicted when the frustrated *Guardia Civil* officer who had ordered his execution hit him with a rifle butt.

As the well-armed party guarding Blanco passed the open fields, peasants came near to see who had been captured. The word spread swiftly across the fields. More peasants appeared,

Blanco's captors walked faster and faster, their fear of the
assembling peasants growing with each step. When they arrived at the small town, a crowd gathered. Although Blanco
had never organized in that town, and although the peasant
unions were not popular there, people began to express their
solidarity.

Shouts of "Land or Death" and "Long Live Hugo Blanco"
rose in the streets of this small Andean town. Soon these words
would resound through the valleys and mountains of Peru,
and even beyond its borders.

Fearing the local population, the police called in a helicopter
and rushed Blanco off to the central army barracks in Cuzco.

Blanco refers in this book to the general strike that began
soon after his capture, but he modestly omits its first demand:
Freedom for Hugo Blanco.

Peru's ruling class was torn between a desire to execute
Blanco and their fear of the effect a trial would have on the
masses. They hesitated and sought instead to break Blanco
and the hundreds of other imprisoned peasant militants and
leaders. Blanco was held in solitary confinement for three
years.

The government then rewrote the law so as to place Blanco
under the jurisdiction of a military rather than civil court.
When they brought him to trial, almost four years after his
capture, they did not dare hold it in a major city. Instead
they moved the trial to Tacna, a remote town on the border
between Peru and Chile.

An important additional factor entered into the trial of Blanco
and twenty-eight other peasant leaders in Tacna. The Fourth
International, of which Hugo Blanco is a member, organized
an international defense campaign for him and his fellow prisoners. Members and supporters of the Fourth International
joined with other supporters of democratic rights, of all kinds
of political persuasions and organizations, in organizing as
wide a protest as possible.

Participation in the defense campaign was based on only
one point of agreement—justice for political prisoners. The
committees set up to further this work did not take positions
on any other matter; they expressed neither agreement nor
disagreement with the political views of the defendants. With
this approach, the committees were able to reach out to people
who disagreed politically with Blanco but who were against
the injustice of the prosecution. The result was immense international pressure on the Peruvian government.

In Santiago, Chile, the entire Chamber of Deputies voted

to ask Belaúnde, then the president of Peru, for amnesty for Blanco. Illiterate peasants in Arauco, Chile, signed petitions for Blanco's freedom with their thumbprints.

In Argentina, the union Blanco had belonged to, along with many other unions, sent messages of support. The national secretary of the Italian Confederation of Labor sent a petition to Belaúnde. In Belgium, forty-three members of parliament called for his release.

Sugar workers in the state of Bihar in India and 7,000 trade unionists in French Canada joined with Parisian schoolteachers and London engineers in protesting the Peruvian prosecutor's demand for the death sentence.

Isaac Deutscher, Jean-Paul Sartre, Simone de Beauvoir, the International League for Human Rights, Amnesty International, ten British MPs, Bertrand Russell, four hundred scholars in the United States, political prisoners in Mexico, and countless others joined in the international campaign for amnesty.

Mass demonstrations of tens of thousands in Peru itself reinforced the impact of the international effort. The hand of the executioner was stayed. But Blanco was not freed. The military, acting as judge, jury, and prosecutor, sentenced him to twenty-five years imprisonment. Hugo Blanco appealed this harsh sentence. The military, in a counterappeal, again demanded the death sentence. This new threat to Blanco's life created a most serious situation. In Peru, death sentences are carried out within twenty-four hours of the verdict.

It was under these conditions, awaiting the decision of the top generals, that Hugo Blanco wrote his moving letter to the students of Peru, which is included in this volume. The sentence of twenty-five years was upheld, and Blanco was transferred to the infamous island prison, El Frontón, off the coast of Callao.

A comrade and close friend of Blanco, the Argentine, Eduardo Creus, was also imprisoned in El Frontón on a seventeen-year sentence. Aided by Creus, Blanco was able to continue to help the struggle of the working people of Peru from his prison cell. His articles denouncing the government, supporting strikes, and exposing the mistreatment of other political prisoners kept appearing in Peru and other countries. When the guerrilla fighters of the MIR (Movimiento de Izquierda Revolucionaria) and other groups were imprisoned, Hugo Blanco, although critical of their political views, came to their defense, urging all Peruvians to protest their brutal treatment.

Although it directly endangered his own life, Blanco continuously exposed the treatment of prisoners in El Frontón.

On September 12, 1968, for instance, the magazine *Ojo* published a report from Hugo Blanco describing how two prisoners at El Frontón had been slowly beaten to death. Locked up in a place the prisoners called the "House of Dracula," the guards took turns beating the prisoners with clubs from morning until evening, when they died. In his article, Blanco named the murderers, three captains, two lieutenants, two sergeants, and a corporal of the *Guardia Republicana*.

In an attempt to cover up the murders and facilitate further reprisals on prisoners, the guards attempted to provoke the prisoners into a mutiny. They forced them to pass over foul ramps covered with excrement on their way to meals and visits with their families.

In October 1968, the military overthrew Belaúnde and established the "Revolutionary Government of the Armed Forces." This new government, led by Juan Velasco Alvarado, declared itself in favor of an agrarian reform and other reforms of a nationalistic nature. But the new "revolutionary government" did not see fit to release the prisoners whose only crime had been to fight for a thoroughgoing agrarian reform. It might be added that it also chose not to change conditions in the prisons. On December 13, 1968, Blanco again wrote an open letter describing the torture of prisoners, especially political prisoners.

Of course, Velasco's land reform is quite different from the one carried out in Chaupimayo. The primary aim of the Velasco regime is to improve the general well-being of the capitalist system in Peru. The well-being of the workers and peasants is of secondary concern. Some of the reforms of the Velasco regime, however, aimed at modernizing the economy, have benefited the peasants and workers. Blanco urged the people to take full advantage of these reforms and to press for their own direct participation and decision-making in the implementation of each change. This, of course, is unacceptable to the Velasco regime.

With the new "left" rhetoric of the government, there were rumors that the political prisoners would be freed. In fact, the regime began to take a friendly attitude to the very same people it had itself imprisoned or was holding in prison. Before long, it became evident that the Velasco regime, seeking popular support, wanted to buy the allegiance of the left in Peru in order to leave the masses leaderless and unable to mobilize to protect their own interests.

The Communist Party was among the first to capitulate. It began to give full support to the military dictatorship. Soon after, other left groups and individuals capitulated.

As a part of this maneuver, and in response to international pressure, Velasco declared a general amnesty for political prisoners in December 1970, two years after assuming power. The amnesty declared all political prisoners freed. In reality, only some were freed. Hugo Blanco had to be included among those freed, or the decree would have been obviously phony and without impact.

So, suddenly, after almost eight years of imprisonment, on December 22, 1970, Hugo Blanco found himself free. Other well-known political prisoners were also released.

The campaign by the Velasco regime to coopt the left continued to meet with success. Héctor Béjar, the guerrilla leader and Havana literary prize-winner, capitulated. In return, he got a job with the government in the *Movilización Social.* Ismael Frías, for many years a leading Peruvian Trotskyist, capitulated. In return, he has a soft job writing a daily column attacking the workers, peasants, and students who protest against Velasco's military dictatorship.

It was an open secret in Peru that the Velasco regime would pay lavishly in return for Hugo Blanco's capitulation. For his popularity in Peru is unparalleled. If Blanco were to declare support for the Velasco regime, it would give the regime great moral authority, especially among the peasants.

But when Blanco addressed the ten thousand in Lima who gathered to welcome him and other political prisoners upon their release, he declared, as always, that there could be no compromise with injustice, with the denial of democratic rights, with the denial of land to those who work it, or with the semicolonial status of Peru which permits American imperialism to drain its wealth.

Most shocking of all to the Velasco regime was Hugo Blanco's call for the release of dozens of other political prisoners, including his own comrade Eduardo Creus, who remained behind bars. This exposed the Velasco's claim that there were no more political prisoners in Peru.

Blanco interrupted his own speech to introduce a peasant leader to the mass gathering. He told how, in the name of land reform, Velasco was forcing peasants who had carried out their own land reform eight years earlier to pay the former proprietors for the land the peasants had worked all their lives. The peasant leader explained that in spite of their poverty, they had come from the interior provinces, sleeping at night on the freezing ground, to discuss their grievances with the "revolutionary government," and that the government officials had refused even to meet with them.

The pressure brought to bear by Blanco was reflected a

month later when the government released Eduardo Creus,
deporting him to his native Argentina.

The people of Cuzco began preparations for a huge welcome-
home gathering for Hugo Blanco. But Velasco stepped in
and prohibited him from leaving Lima. The minister of the
interior, General Armando Artola, explained to the press that
Hugo Blanco was a fine person and that the government
feared that someone might hurt Blanco in Cuzco — so the pro-
hibition on his travel was "for his own protection."

Confined to Lima, Blanco declared that he would violate
no laws. He concentrated on publicizing the situation of the
other political prisoners, especially of poor peasants in the
interior. But the Velasco regime was nervous. It could not
tolerate the presence of one who could not be bought, of one
who had the trust of the masses. At first, the government sent
emissaries who indicated that Blanco would be awarded a
government post if he would cooperate. Blanco, always po-
lite, simply declined the invitation. Instead, he continued to
meet and discuss with peasants, workers, students, trade unionists, and reporters who visited his home. Then the government
arrested him in retaliation and held him for twenty-four hours
of hard questioning.

Every time workers went on strike or peasants struggled
for improved conditions, the right-wing press would scream,
"Hugo Blanco Is At It Again." Although Blanco's organization,
the FIR, began to grow again, primarily among workers in
Lima, it still remains a relatively small group. But the para-
noia of the ruling class in Peru tends to see Blanco's hand
behind every effort of the masses to improve their conditions.

In September 1971, only nine months after his release, a
militant teachers' strike swept Peru. The masses supported
the strike. Demonstrations broke out. The government sent the
police to smash the strike and hundreds were arrested.

About this time, Hugo Blanco had helped Rosa Alarco,
a tireless defender of Peruvian political prisoners, to gather
the signatures of 400 well-known Peruvians and others to a
statement demanding the release of political prisoners still in
jail. The petition listed the name of each prisoner and the
prison he or she was held in. It also referred to the decree
of general amnesty, which has the status of law in Peru. Thus
all that Blanco and the petitioners were demanding was that
Velasco live up to his own law.

Without explanation, the police suddenly arrested Blanco
in his home at 8:00 p.m. on September 13, 1971. Since no
formal charges were made, it could best be described as kid-

napping. Blanco was held for twenty-four hours and then deported. In a CIA-like operation, his destination was concealed from the world press by the Velasco government. The Peruvian government waited two days after deporting Blanco to Mexico to announce that they had deported him to Panama. A number of the leaders of the teachers' union were also arrested and deported.

In Mexico, the authorities held Hugo Blanco until they could ascertain his status. They then permitted him to stay as a resident alien. He is now living in exile in Mexico City.

Peter Camejo
October 23, 1971

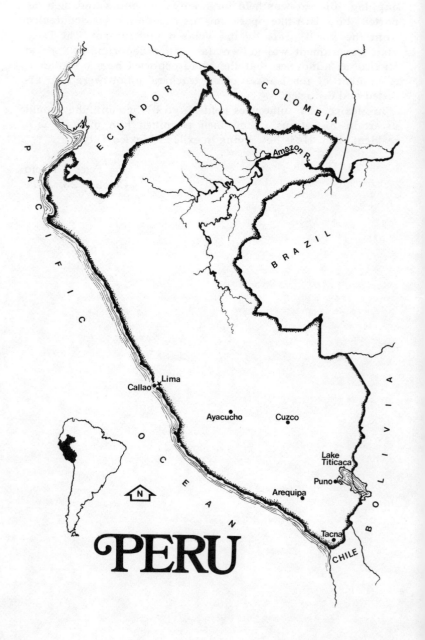

ECUADOR

COLOMBIA

P A C I F I C

Amazon R.

B R A Z I L

Lima
Callao

Ayacucho

Cuzco

O C E A N

Lake
Titicaca

Puno

B O L I V I A

Arequipa

N

Tacna

PERU

CHILE

1

The Sequence of Events

A serious Trotskyist organization has existed in Peru since 1946, the year in which the recently formed Marxist Workers Group (Grupo Obrero Marxista — GOM) constituted itself as the Revolutionary Workers Party (Partido Obrero Revolucionario — POR), Peruvian section of the Fourth International.

The leaders of the early period were Paco Abril, Félix Zevallos, Carlos Howes, Ismael Frías, Hernando Aguirre, among others. This heroic early stage was concluded with the repression carried out in 1952 by General Odría.[1] Most of the Trotskyists were jailed or exiled. The great crisis in the world Trotskyist movement during that period had an impact on the exiles, and when they returned to Peru after eight oppressive years, two POR's emerged: one was led by Frías and influenced by the Pablo and Posadas tendency;[2] the other, whose best-known leader was Félix Zevallos, belonged to the tendency which at that time called itself orthodox, and was strongly influenced by the Argentine Trotskyist party. It was in that party, among whose leaders Nahuel Moreno particularly stood out, that I acquired my Marxist education.

The POR emerged as an expression of the necessity for a truly revolutionary workers' party in the context of the treachery of the so-called leftist parties of that period: the American Popular Revolutionary Alliance (Alianza Popular Revolucionaria Americana — APRA)[3] and the Peruvian Communist Party. The POR was formed by revolutionaries who understood that those parties were beyond reform and that the independent organization of a real party of the Peruvian revolution was essential. Unfortunately, at the beginning of the second stage, the faction led by Frías began to retreat from this concept, began to lose confidence in the ability and potential of the Peruvian revolution to form its own party directly. It projected entry into APRA as the principal task. (It said, in addition, that in Cuzco[4] and in some other places it was necessary to enter the Communist Party and in the North, the Socialist Party.)

The other faction maintained the original position of the

POR: to build the revolutionary party independently. It pointed to the principal task, which was to promote and advance the struggles the working class was developing through its trade unions, to raise them higher and higher, to organize a revolutionary trade-union tendency which could bring together the best trade-union leaders and activists. It expected that the revolutionary party would be formed in this struggle. This was the faction that published the newspaper *POR* and which, after more than a year of purely working-class organizing, began to do peasant organizing in 1958.

That peasant campaign, in which I played an active role from 1958 to 1963, is the central theme of this work. I present here a chronological summary of the peasant organizing of this period from its beginning until I was captured. I believe this summary is necessary to convey a clear idea of the sequence of events that I shall describe in the following chapters.

To be quite honest, we must recognize that we did not begin our peasant organizing because we had a clear political picture beforehand of the importance of the peasantry in our country; rather, it was largely a result of the pressure of circumstances. In addition, the theoretical contributions of Comrade Nahuel Moreno, in particular, helped tremendously in making us conscious of that importance.

The visit of Richard Nixon, then vice-president of the United States, to Lima in 1958 provoked mass protest demonstrations on such a scale that the repressive forces were taken by surprise. Afterwards, they reacted by lashing out against the revolutionary groups; the POR, which had been one of the principal leaders of the demonstrations, was also one of the groups that suffered the harshest repression. With the object of preventing my capture, it was agreed that I should leave the factory where I was working, where I had not yet been admitted into the union because I had not been working there three months.

Then, taking into account among other factors the great combativity being displayed by the people of Cuzco (going beyond their leadership, they had taken control of practically the entire city in April 1958), the party sent me to that city. I was the most obvious person to send there because I was a native of that department and was also unemployed.

In arranging this, the party did so not with the intention of opening up a peasant organizing campaign, but was still thinking about urban organizing. Naturally, we figured that my first step was to become a member of the Cuzco Workers Federation (FTC), where I would find the most militant of the workers. I arrived at the federation headquarters in the capacity of delegate from the Amalgamated Union of Newspaper Retailers, whose formation I had led.

Inside the FTC, I came up against a reality that we had not expected: it was basically an organization of artisans, with minority representation of workers. In addition, its radical wing was composed not of workers' representatives but of peasant delegates. It was then that I began my peasant campaign; for, although the militants of the POR had what was for Peru a lopsided orientation toward the urban working class, still, as Marxists, we followed the practice of examining reality and assimilating its lessons, and then taking action along a revolutionary path.

The peasant unions of La Convención, which began forming under Odría, became more numerous under Prado.[5] I joined one of them, the Peasant Union of Chaupimayo, in the capacity of subtenant (below a tenant farmer and below a freeholder). This union was the bulwark of revolutionary opposition to the bureaucracy that ran the FTC and its followers. These bureaucrats emphatically rejected my nomination as the union's delegate to the FTC, and nearly threw me out of the federation. They also used all their resources to block me from participating directly in organizing the Provincial Peasants Federation of La Convención (FPCC) at the founding congress of this group and in its assemblies. Nevertheless, nothing could prevent me from participating indirectly.

I subsequently went to Lima as a union delegate to the Confederation of Peruvian Peasants, and there I got a broader picture of the peasant movement.

In the course of the FPCC's first year of existence, the revolutionary current became so much stronger that the second secretary-general to be elected was Andrés Gonzales, one of the leaders of Chaupimayo, who belonged to the POR.

In 1960, when I returned to Cuzco after a stay of a few months in Lima, I was jailed for having led a picket line the previous year in a city strike that had resulted in a skirmish with the police. After more than two months in prison, I declared a hunger strike for the first time, this time to demand my liberty. The revolutionary peasantry helped in other ways, by pressuring the FTC to such an extent that the bureaucrats eventually felt compelled to demand my release by threatening a work stoppage — a tactic that proved successful. From that moment on, it was impossible for the bureaucrats to prevent my direct participation in the FPCC and FTC assemblies. In the FPCC, I took on the duties of first under-secretary and later on secretary of press and publicity, although my basic occupation was organizing and reorganizing unions and their struggles.

The peasantry in the valleys of La Convención and Lares (united in the FPCC) was little by little radicalizing its struggle, with strikes, work stoppages and meetings, disregarding judicial eviction notices, and so forth.

Subsequently, the Departmental Peasants Federation of Cuzco (FDCC) was organized. At its founding congress, our disagreements with the opportunists became sharper.

A political event of importance during this period was the constitution of the Revolutionary Left Front (Frente de Izquierda Revolucionario — FIR) in Cuzco, which united the local revolutionary left. Subsequently, the FIR was organized on a national level.

The arrival in Cuzco of comrades Antonio Aragón, "Che" Pereyra, Gorki Tapia, and Héctor Loayza, who were sent by the party, significantly strengthened our peasant organizing, especially in the preparation for armed struggle, which until that time was only just beginning.

At this time, the bank expropriations, carried out in Lima with the object of obtaining funds for arming the peasantry of Cuzco, triggered a fierce repression which almost destroyed the FIR.

My election late in April 1962 as secretary-general of the Provincial Federation against the rabid opposition of the opportunists coincided with the beginning of a wholesale persecution. Despite this persecution, I was able to remain active, although in a restricted way, thanks to the massive support of the peasants.

Even though the opportunists of the Communist Party were strengthened by the repression against us, the class contradictions grew sharper each day between April and November, and culminated in the beginning of the armed struggle.

The almost complete absence of an adequate political apparatus on a national or even a local scale, and the geographical limitations of the movement as a consequence, were the fundamental causes of the defeat of the incipient armed struggle and the corresponding partial retreat by the peasantry, with the relative strengthening of the reaction and of Stalinist opportunism.

Under those conditions, my capture took place in May 1963.

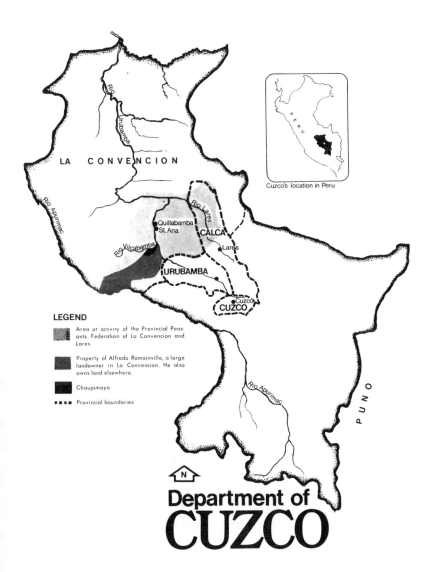

Cuzco's location in Peru

LA CONVENCION

Rio Urubamba

Rio Apurimac

Rio Lares

Quillabamba
St. Ana

CALCA

Rio Vilcabamba

Lares

URUBAMBA

Cuzco
CUZCO

P U N O

Rio Apurimac

LEGEND

Area of activity of the Provincial Peasants Federation of La Convencion and Lares

Property of Alfredo Romainville, a large landowner in La Convencion. He also owns land elsewhere.

Chaupimayo

■■■■ Provincial boundaries

N

Department of
CUZCO

2
The Geographical, Economic, and Social Setting

The scene of the struggles described in this book is the department of Cuzco in the southern mountians of Peru. The basic action developed in the zones of La Convención and Lares. In this department there are high peaks perpetually covered with snow. (Some are more than 6,000 meters [19,685 feet] above sea level.) Beneath these peaks lies the region known as the *puna* [grass covered, windswept plains]. It is a frigid zone, generally without rain.

In the *puna* live the Andean people, the Quechua Indians, [1] who devote themselves to animal husbandry and farming. The basic crop is potatoes. In addition they raise *oca* [a sorrel with edible tuberous roots], *olluco* [a vine with edible tuberous roots], and *quinoa* [a pigweed whose seeds are ground up and used as cereal]. Beans and other produce are grown in lesser quantities.

The animal husbandry consists fundamentally of egg farming and cattle ranching. The alpaca, an aboriginal animal related to the camel, is raised in smaller numbers, mostly in the highest zones. The beasts of burden are horses and burros. The llama, another member of the camel family, is more useful as a beast of burden than for its wool or flesh. The vicuña, also related to the camel, is not domesticated. This species is on its way to extinction; it has very highly valued wool. Hunting it is forbidden by law, but the big landowners and the Civil Guards are consenting to the extinction of this species. Export of vicuña wool is forbidden, but it is regularly exported to Europe and the United States.

Continuing the eastward descent, one finds zones that are less frigid, but still mostly without rain. In these zones wheat is the staple crop, and to a lesser extent beans and barley. Besides the crops of the *puna,* there are others, *tarwi* [the fruit of a leguminous plant], green peas, and chick peas.

Lower still, in the more temperate zones, less afflicted with ice and having an adequate rainfall, maize is cultivated. However, the zones where maize predominates are already the ravines, the valleys with heavy rainfalls. Since the above-named

crops can be cultivated in regions without rain, the irrigated
regions of the ravines are used mostly for maize and also for
potatoes, which are grown out of season to command a higher
price. Beans, fruits, and green vegetables are also more com-
monly grown in this region. It is rare to find *quinoa* or other
crops proper to the *puna* being farmed here.

As for animal husbandry, the greater the descent from the
highlands, the greater the proportion of cattle farming, and the
less egg farming and goat farming; also the pack animals native
to the *puna* become increasingly scarce. The proportion of
pigs, hens, guinea pigs, ducks, and other livestock increases.

Up to the temperate zone, we are in sierra, properly named,
with its mixed and varied subregions formed by the rivers
that crisscross the Andes in every direction. When the rivers
swell, they flow east, toward the Amazonian plain, toward
the great river itself. In this eastward descent, the forested slopes
and ridges form the anteroom to the Amazonian rainforest.

In the department of Cuzco, these transitional geographic
areas are called "the valleys." The Quechua peasants call them
the *yunka*. The inhabitants of these zones call the rest of the
department, from the *puna* to the temperate ravines, the "outside."
The Indian lived "outside" for centuries. The *yunka*, "inside," is
not his world, but is a colonized zone, a zone of immigration.
The natives of this region are the *Chunchos,* primitive tribes that
have been massacred or driven into the interior of the Amazonian *selva.* These zones are torrid.

The valleys of La Convención and Lares were the principal
scene of the events that are the subject of this book. The valley
of La Convención is formed by the Vilcanota River (*Willcamayu*),
also called the *Urubamba.* The valley of Lares is formed by
one of the tributaries of the Vilcanota, the Yanatile River.

Agriculturally, the fundamental difference between these hot
valleys and the mountainous region derives from the predominantly continous, rather than annual, crops in the valleys.
This characteristic has had a great influence on the economic
and social life of the zone.

The principal crops are coffee, coca, tea, cacao, and such
fruits as bananas, oranges, papayas, and mangoes. To a
lesser extent, *achiote* [seed of the annatto tree used for making
dyes], peanuts, and others. The cultivation of maize is basically
for consumption, as is that of *uncucha* [a plant with fragrant
white flowers whose roots are edible]. On the other hand, yucca
is grown as much for consumption as for trade; the same with
bananas, which are usually eaten boiled.

The agricultural production of the Cuzco sierra is utilized principally for the farmers' consumption and for trade within the department. The production on the forested slopes is mostly for export to other sections of the country, and even to other countries.

The prices of the sierra products are low. Prices for products of the slopes of the *selva* are generally higher; though they suffer from the wide fluctuations of the world market, they are always well above the prices of the sierra products.

In the sierra the crops are annual. On the forested slopes and valleys, most of them grow the year round. First, several years of great sacrifices in every sense are required and then the results are plantations and various installations which come under the heading of "improvements." This difference determines that, while in the sierra the investment of capital and labor bears fruit in an immediate, annual way, on the slopes of the *selva* the rewards are gathered over a long term, with the lean years followed by the fat years.

The sacrifices that the first years on the ridges and valleys of the *selva* demand of the colonizers, who convert the inhospitable entanglement into cultivated land, are in general proportionately greater for those who come from the sierra. These people — from another climate, from another way of life, after centuries on the frigid or temperate sierra, on the lands cultivated by their ancestors since time immemorial, with great suffering and difficulty — find themselves obliged by a new way of life to change their customs, their diet, their life style, their dress. Unlike the *Chunchos* of the *selva* tribe, they are not natives of the zone. They are transplants who even after several generations still maintain much of the sierra culture. The centuries weigh heavily, especially among the peasantry, which is the most conservative sector in its customs.

In the Cuzco sierra, the predominant forms of production are those of the indigenous communal village, or *ayllu,* and its opposite, the hacienda and the latifundia. These are mixed or intermediary formations. The *ayllu* is the peasant commune, which owns the land it works. It is the cell of primitive communism that has survived the Inca Empire, the Colonial period, and the Republic.

The Inca Empire arranged the *ayllu* for the benefit of the exploiters. The colonialists dealt it serious blows. The Republic tried to liquidate it, but failed; although it did succeed in weakening it significantly. Bolívar and other statesmen declared it "dissolved," an analysis that was later modified. At present, Pedro Beltrán[2] (chief of the commission on agrarian reform during the Prado era) is openly proposing its liquidation. Other administrations, for instance, the current military junta, try to liquidate it in disguised ways, attacking its protectors or its modernizers.

The communal, collectivist system of the *ayllu* has, to be sure, deteriorated fundamentally in the face of advancing capitalism. Nevertheless, the *ayllus* maintain many communal features. Although the private ownership of plots is now generally established, the *ayllu* still makes efforts to prevent the sale of land to outsiders and to redistribute uncultivated land. The annual redivision of the plots of *puna* set aside for potatoes and other crops of this zone is still practiced on a large scale. The natural pasture lands are collectively owned. Work is collective. The contribution of work is reciprocal — work is reimbursed with work (*ayni*). Work for the common benefit is carried out collectively. The communal organization is preserved, although every day it deteriorates more because of official regulation.

The *ayllu* is acquiring strength with the revolutionary upsurge; it rediscovers itself. It is possible that the *ayllu* will become one of the basic forms of the future workers' and peasants' government.

The hacienda is the latifundia brought in by the Spanish Conquest. It was not affected by Independence. Bolívar and other liberation fighters were large landowners. The generals of the War of Independence were rewarded with haciendas at the expense of the Indians.

The haciendas, the latifundias, grew at the expense of the peasants' communal villages, seizing lands with the facade of legality — or without it. The hacienda is a vast expanse of land that is partially cultivated in an extensive form.

In the pre-Inca and Inca periods, cultivation had an intensive character, and arable land was well looked after. Graded terraces were constructed to protect the small amount of arable land on the Andean slopes against soil erosion; fertile topsoil was even transported considerable distances.

The conquistadores, during the Colonial period, and their heirs in the epoch of the Republic took it upon themselves to destroy the terraces and to murder the soil, even as they murdered the people. (In the Colonial epoch, there were wholesale slaughters of Indians.) The conquistadores, who were fundamentally prospectors, had many hills to plow, and didn't have to worry; when they exhausted one hill, they had another one plowed, always in a murderously extensive fashion. That method was followed by the large landowners of the Republic, the *gamonales,* who no longer even had the excuse of being prospectors.

The large landowner gives a parcel of land to the peasant to work for himself. As rental payment for this parcel, the peasant, the "hacienda Indian," is obliged to work the fields of the landowner. This feudal-type relationship is complemented by other duties for the peasant: unpaid labor on construction, on roads (*faena*), on transportation of produce (*propio*), domestic work in the landlord's house (*pongo*). Many of these duties are imposed on members of the peasant's family.

For the privilege of keeping livestock, which the peasants nurture and fatten on the local pastures, they have to surrender some animals to the lord (*yerbaje*), and at times must also pay with labor. The peasants' pack animals are used at will by the landlord, without payment.

The haciendas have grown continually at the expense of the communal villages. Others have been born in recent periods. This, and the population expansion of the communal villages, has converted many *comuneros* into tenant farmers; sometimes this is true of entire villages. The "hacienda Indian," then, retains many of his *comunero* features. There are also those who are both *comuneros* and tenants.

To the extent that capitalism has penetrated the countryside, it has gradually modified some features of this agrarian situation characterized by the hacienda and the communal village. More advanced relations of production are to be found: exchange payments made in money; "division of labor," in which the landowner contributes the seed and the peasant, the work, and the crop is shared; minifundia, worked directly by owners; wage labor. Multiple combinations of these forms also occur in different degrees.

Nevertheless, at the outset of the peasant movement in Cuzco, the predominant agrarian reality was, on one hand, the backward latifundia with feudal relations and, on the other hand, the village. The conflict presented itself fundamentally as the struggle of the *comuneros* to recover the lands which had been seized from them relatively recently and the struggle of the "hacienda Indians" for the reduction of obligations required in return for the parcels of land they occupied; and sometimes for the right to stay on that land, now that the penetration of capitalism was stimulating the landowner to evict them.

Many aspects of this reality were definitely forbidden by law, even by the constitution. But juridical laws cannot pre-

Panorama of the city of Cuzco

Cyclopean masonry of ancient Inca ruins, used here as the foundation for a relatively new building.

A street scene in Cuzco showing the Arch of San Francisco

vail over economic laws, and still less over the relation of
forces between classes. In many cases even laws "favorable" to the peasantry have been used against them.

This is the economic aspect of the relations. But there is
more. The Indian is an oppressed nationality. Although the
wall separating the Indians from the *mestizos* (those of mixed,
that is, Spanish and Indian, ancestry) and the whites is not
as solid as in the case of the Afro-Americans and the whites
in the United States, their humiliation and oppression are
worse. Their language, their music, their manner of dress,
their tastes, and their customs are ridiculed, suppressed, and
denigrated.

Gonzales Prada[3] spoke of a "social race," more than a
"race of blood descent." And this is certain, for there are
"Indians" of Indian language, Indian dress, Indian customs,
who are white by birth (for example, in Pillpinto); and there
have been gentlemen of Indian descent in the Government
Palace. Nevertheless, these exceptions are not sufficient to refute the existence of the Indian as an oppressed nationality,
and they do not justify subsuming the Indian problem ex-
clusively under the general economic problem.

Without question, the struggle in the countryside is between
the peasant and the *gamonales;* but the resurgence of the
Indian, of the oppressed nationality, is a fundamental ingred-
ient. Therefore, we always spoke Quechua throughout the
struggle, and always exalted everything Indian. The Indians,
exploited not only by the big landowners, but also by the
authorities and by the well-to-do *mestizos,* rose up against
all their exploitation.

The valleys of La Convención and Lares were in the hands
of the great owners of the "wastelands" [the forested transitional area between the highlands and the Amazon basin]. The
landowners had obtained them as gifts in the Colonial period.
During the Republican period, the means of obtaining the
latifundias were similar: the future owner (a rich and influential person) claimed (obtained on concession) vast expanses
of land, paying the state ridiculously small sums of money;
he would then avail himself without challenge of even greater
expanses.

If in the sierra the haciendas have increased at the expense
of the lands of the indigenous villages, on the forested slopes
they have increased at the expense of the virgin lands owned
by the state.

The titles to the vast tracts of land that are claimed need

not stipulate that they will be cultivated. On the contrary, the state has determined that these tracts will not be cultivated. Many new claimants with honest intentions of settling had and still have to penetrate deep into the interior at great distances from any outposts of civilization and means of communication, in order to find lands without "owners."

The system of *gamonalismo* has been and is the main obstacle to the colonization of the Peruvian *selva*. If the land had been given to whoever would work it, then, from the first areas of prosperous colonization, new areas would have been easily brought into cultivation, without great sacrifice and with high productivity.

But it would be absurd to expect such a thing from a government which represents precisely those *gamonales* and other exploitative sectors, and not the great majority of Peruvian people. Even the present government, representing the pro-development bourgeois sectors, native and imperialist, is showing itself capable of effective steps in this respect because of the mutual ties that unite all the exploiting sectors.

The serious and effective incorporation of the *selva* into the national economy is one more task that will fall upon the future workers' and peasants' government. The exploiting classes, including the so-called progressive bourgeoisie, which has been so glorified by the Stalinists, have shown themselves to be incapable of accomplishing this bourgeois task.

The *gamonales* of La Convención and Lares transferred to these valleys the relations of production and the system of exploitation that prevailed in the sierra. The peasants were immigrants from other zones of the department, and even from other departments. The landowner gave to the peasant "tenant" a tract of virgin *selva* to farm for himself. To pay their rent, the tenants had to work a specified number of days for the landowner, and in some cases had to pay a certain sum of money besides. They had additional obligations such as the labor of women and children (*palla*), labor without pay on roads, canals, and so forth. In some haciendas, the tenants were obliged in turn to pay all the workers who labored on the hacienda on specific days. Finally, such sierra customs as the *propios,* the *yerbaje,* and even a certain type of *pongaje* [domestic service in the landlord's house] were imported to the valleys of La Convención and Lares.

With the increase of year-round crops, there was a vast increase in the need for farmhands. The landowners imposed more conditions, and the tenant had to spend more time attending to his own plot (*arriendo*). Thus arose the institution of the subtenant, often a relative or friend of the tenant, to whom the tenant assigns a small parcel of land within his own, imposing on him the obligation of payment in days of work, much like that imposed on him by the landowners.

The enemies of the peasant movement, especially the landowners, used to say that the real exploiter was the tenant. This was false; in reality the obligation of work imposed on the subtenants was absorbed by working for the landowner and came nowhere near covering the tenant's obligations. For example, a tenant might have a principal obligation to work fourteen days a month for the landlord, and might have three subtenants, each one of whom had the obligation to work three days a month for him; he cannot begin to cover the fourteen days with the sum of their time. The cases of a tenant coming out ahead with this system are very rare.

This could be seen clearly in the united front the unions formed. The victories that the tenants were gradually winning (a decrease in the obligations due the landlord, looking ultimately to their total annulment) were reflected immediately in the condition of the subtenants, with satisfaction in both sectors.

It was precisely the "exceptional tenants" who were the principal strikebreakers.

On rare occasions there occurred the sub-subtenant, who bore the same relation to the subtenant that the latter bore to the tenant. Besides these layers, there were the agricultural laborers, wage workers who were brought from the sierra. These laborers generally went to the valleys only temporarily, usually around the harvest, their real center of work being in the sierra. When they remained in the valleys, they generally became subtenants.

Thanks to the superior economic yield of the crops of the zone and to the value that the plantations acquired, the contradictions in the region sharpened.

The *gamonales* not only demanded more and more of the tenants (and even of the subtenants), but their chief desire was to evict the tenants and subtenants and to possess themselves the plantations in their entirety. The tenants and the subtenants, in their turn, wanted the landlords to ease conditions and guarantee their right to stay on their little plots of land.

In many cases, the *gamonales* accomplished their aims and succeeded in taking the plantations entirely away from the peasants, sometimes using judges and courts, and other times without need of them. These actions cost the life of landowner Alberto Duque, who fell in an ambush prepared by four peasants who were desperate and powerless before the arrogantly biased "justice" that was attempting to steal their land.

This sharpening of contradictions spurred the unionization of the peasantry in the zone. The peasant unions were organized almost completely by tenants and subtenants. The agricultural laborers, because they were migratory laborers who came only intermittently to the zone, took very little interest in the union. When they did show some interest in it, it was with regard to the problems of their own regions. They were an important factor in extending unionism to other zones, just as the tenants and subtenants were when they made trips back to their native areas.

Through the initiative of the vanguard of tenants and subtenants, and not through the action of the transient laborers themselves, some benefits were achieved for the laborers, guaranteeing them a minimum wage and otherwise protecting them from abuses. During the strongest period of the union movement, those laborers who so desired were given plots of land.

We knew that the exploitation of the agricultural laborers would end only when the sierra land belonged to those who worked it; so the laborers were justified in putting their main interest in transmitting the seeds of unionism and even in participating along with tenants and subtenants in the struggle against the *gamonales.*

The most well-to-do sectors of the tenants, among whom the Communist Party had its principal roots, saw this and considered it a danger for themselves. Therefore, they preferred a compromise solution between landlords and tenants. They realized that the appropriation without payment by tenants and subtenants of the plots they occupied, and the distribution of virgin lands to whoever wanted to farm them, would set off a chain reaction that would not stop at the village limits, but would affect their future hiring of agricultural laborers.

We explained the great possibilities of peasant ownership of the land which would utilize collective labor in a rational way, as well as technology and science, so that the labor of one man would produce what now requires the labor of many.

In Quillabamba, the capital of the province, and in other towns, the poor workers and the lower middle classes were with the peasantry. The Shopkeepers Union participated actively in important mobilizations.

The rich merchants and other wealthy sectors were against

us because of their connections with the *gamonales* and because it made their blood boil to see the Indian, for whom they had always had contempt, transformed into the proud master of the province. The prospect of the advent of cooperatives, which would replace the merchants, also influenced their attitudes.

The teachers, caught up at the beginning in the petty-bourgeois environment, later came over to the side of the peasantry. This happened when the peasants displayed tremendous solidarity with a historic teachers' strike, at the very moment when the petty-bourgeois sectors, our enemies, were chiming in with the exploiters' vilification of the strike.

Consequently, at the time of the peasantry's greatest strength, the urban center of Santa María, under the leadership of the peasant vanguard and with the massive support of the peasantry, proceeded to divide up some *urban* property that belonged to a big landowner. This produced cries of outrage and public denunciation by the Stalinists, but it won us the loyalty of the population of Santa María and the sympathy of other urban sectors.

At the height of the peasant uprising, tenants and subtenants made themselves the owners of their plots of land. In addition, on some haciendas the fields of the landowner were collectivized. The peasants also proceeded to distribute virgin lands among those who wanted to farm them.

As a consequence of governmental repression, the process was frustrated and in some aspects set back: the leased and subleased land remained in the hands of the peasants, but the fields of the landowners were returned, and work on the new acreage prevented.

Chaupimayo, where the fields of the landlord remained in peasant hands and some new lands were plowed, is one of the exceptions. The government did not dare impose a stricter repression there because of the imminent danger of insurrection.

The present military junta, with more persistence than the previous junta and the government of Belaúnde,[4] has tried to legalize the peasants' possession of leased and subleased land by means of installment payments by the peasants to the landowners via the government. This effort by the present government is a response not only to its fear of insurrection, but also to its stake, as a representative of business and industry, in capitalist development in the countryside.

The peasantry, on the whole, is refusing to pay for the land which it won in struggle against nature, the *gamonales*, and the government. This illegal, but de facto, possession annoys the government. If it were only a question of La Convención and Lares, they would legalize possession without payment. But the government knows that the big landowners would certainly declare that it was setting a dangerous precedent. It would be tantamount to legalizing the revolutionary methods of the masses. And the government distinguishes very clearly between its self-proclaimed revolutionary title[5] and its role as guardian of bourgeois order.

It is very difficult to speak from afar of the present class relations in La Convención and Lares. Nevertheless, there are some far-reaching aspects that can be mentioned.

As we have said, the contradiction between the government and the peasants is kept alive by the government's attempt to make them pay for the land, and the peasants' refusal.

Another point of tension has arisen because of the government's creation of marketing cooperatives. It uses these formations to exercise economic domination over the peasantry and to weaken their organizations. The governmental bureaucracy in the zone is tied very closely to the rich landowners and merchants. The peasants are fighting to take control of those cooperatives.

The abolition of serfdom has given impetus to the development of capitalist relations in the zone; the landowners have been obliged not only to adopt the use of modern machinery, but also to hire agricultural workers. This is likewise taking place with some former tenants and even with some former subtenants.

Thus, an agricultural proletariat, less unstable than before, is emerging. This sector of workers will be called upon to play an important role in the future. Many small proprietors, especially former subtenants, are also obliged to work as agricultural wage laborers.

The bourgeoisification of the better-off tenants has come about as a consequence of their abandoning the unions, and this has also strengthened the opportunist current within the union movement. Nevertheless, the peasants as a whole are not disposed to leaving their unions, which have provided them with so many benefits.

La Convención and Lares have overcome feudal servitude and are now in a capitalist phase, but the unity of the former tenants and subtenants remains. It is even possible that the federation will be rejuvenated with the entry of the agricultural laborers and the departure of the better-off tenants. Developments in the movement in La Convención and Lares will be increasingly tied to national developments.

3
The Party

The great deficiency in our work in La Convención and in Cuzco was the absence of a well-organized party. Our failure to broaden the movement, the lack of a more correct view of the process, the putschist deviation of some comrades, the very poor organization of the armed struggle, were symptoms first and foremost of the absence of a party, of a vanguard nucleus whose capabilities would correspond to the magnitude of the peasant movement that developed.

Of course, it was not human material that was lacking, for the evolvement of the peasant struggle in La Convención and in the rest of the department produced its own vanguard, as any struggle does. What was lacking was the distinct organization of that vanguard in a disciplined nucleus, completely conscious of the role it would have to play in the process.

Before beginning its work in Cuzco, the party had shrunk to fewer than ten militants in Lima, and a few more in Arequipa. Furthermore, the POR was a long way from a tempered Bolshevik party. For these reasons, and because we could not see the degree of importance of the peasant campaign, it remained for a long time the field work of only one militant, who was almost completely isolated from the rest of the party.

When we began our work in the countryside, I tried to organize a cell in the city that would be oriented toward peasant organizing. I failed in this attempt; the formation of a cell would have required a lot of work, and I was completely wrapped up in mass peasant organizing.

As for the absence of the party in the countryside, it is indisputable that this was due to a serious syndicalist deviation on my part, produced not by an erroneous conception on this matter, but by other causes:

● The dynamic of the mass movement was powerful and urgent, and completely absorbed me.

● There was no party tradition in the countryside.

● The Stalinist attack was vigorous.

● The classic disadvantage of the peasantry — great distances and isolation.

Because of all this, the revolutionary current in the country-side was no more than that — a current — with Trotskyist features and methodology, but without a formal organization. The central source of this current was the vanguard union Chaupimayo. It was that union that sounded the keynote in moments of upsurge and that was dealt the harshest blows by the reactionaries and the opportunists.

Because of the turbulence created, on one hand, by the *gamonales* and the repression and, on the other, by the Trotskyist vanguard, Chaupimayo became radicalized in such a way that almost all its members became well-disciplined revolutionary trade-union militants. Even rank-and-file members of this union functioned as organizers and leaders in other zones. Chaupimayo was always the vanguard: in the mass mobilizations, in the effort that won power for the peasants, in the preparation for armed struggle, in the militias and in the incipient guerrilla bands. That is why, both in Peru and abroad, the whole peasant movement in the region is identified with the name of Chaupimayo, the focus of Trotskyist action.

Side-by-side with Chaupimayo, there were revolutionary peasant union leaders and activists in the valleys of La Convención and Lares and in other zones of the department of Cuzco.

Occasionally the revolutionary unions held conferences to map out action against the *gamonales* and the opportunists, but they never reached the stage of uniting all of them in a formal organization with regular conventions.

The most outstanding representatives of this tendency were Fortunato Vargas, Andrés Gonzales, Leonidas Carpio, Clemente Andrade, Benigno Valer, and others, from Chaupimayo; Aniceto Muñoz from Pachachaca Grande; Gerardio Carpio, Manuel Delgado and Humberto Carazas from Santa Rosa; Antonio Guevara from Maranura; Benito Cutipa from La Joya; Vicente Lanado from Paltaybamba; Qoyo from San Pablo; Contreras from Tunquimayo; Carmela Giraldo from Huadquiña; Julio Silva from Qollpani Chico; Avelino Almirón from Aranjuez; Vera from Mándor; Lucio Beingolea from Potrero; the Aguilar brothers from Quellomayo; Manuel Canal from Quillabamba.

These leaders of La Convención, together with courageous activists of other provinces who were around the peerless Justo

Huallpa in Cuzco, and those who fought with Claudio Hango
in Lares, have been the real leaders of the process of revolutionary upsurge in La Convención.

I mention names because the vanguard role, in which we
functioned collectively, has been attributed to me alone. It must
be understood that for security reasons I must be silent about
many others who, even now, at a distance of many years
and many jail cells, must not be named. It must also be understood that some have had a change of heart.

In spite of the rabidly anti-Trotskyist propaganda of the
Communist Party, and in spite of the lack of Trotskyist militants in the city, the work in the countryside continually attracted the attention and sympathy of the urban vanguard. It
was this layer that produced the FIR (originally the Revolutionary Front) in Cuzco.

It was composed of the POR, represented on account of our
work in the countryside; the "Communist Party (Leninist)"—a
left group that had broken from the Communist Party and that
had some influence in the workers vanguard—headed by Luis
Zapata Bodero, the terror of the FTC bureaucracy and a hero
of the Peruvian revolution, an unforgettable fighter; part of the
CP youth, with influence among the students; the MIR (Movement of the Revolutionary Left), which was then called APRA
Rebelde[1] of Cuzco—they were with us at first, but when it was
required that all the names of member organizations be printed
in the FIR newsletter, they preferred to leave so as not to
endanger their cordial relations with the Communist Party.

Although organizing the FIR did not directly aid the work in
the countryside, it helped by coordinating it with the urban
work. By that time, the Latin American Secretariat of Orthodox
Trotskyism (SLATO) had realized the great importance of our
peasant movement and the urgent need to strengthen it. They
sent three experienced comrades to our aid: Daniel Pereyra,
Eduardo Creus, and José Martorell—militants of Argentine
Trotskyism. The latter two remained in Lima, and Pereyra
functioned in Lima and Cuzco. The arrival of Pereyra and
other militants of the Peruvian POR in Cuzco strengthened our
work enormously.

The FIR began to grow in Cuzco. It had already been constituted on a national scale. Mass peasant work was intensified
significantly, as much on a provincial scale (La Convención
and Lares) as on a departmental scale (Cuzco). The FIR apparatus in the city, led by Pereyra and Antonio Aragón, en-
ergetically helped the peasant movement, recruiting students

who went to the countryside to organize, printing leaflets and newsletters needed there, and so forth.

In addition, it gave serious impetus to the preparation for armed struggle. Although preparation had begun earlier, it was clearly becoming urgent to step it up in view of the advanced level of the class struggle in the countryside.

Unfortunately, the great deficiency continued to exist: no efforts were made to consolidate the peasant vanguard (tested and proved) into the party or into the FIR, although a few members were recruited incidentally.

The feverish intensification of work without the existence of a solidly formed party required supplementary funds. In Lima, the FIR devoted its efforts to the hasty and indiscriminate recruitment of members. Almost immediately, those new members — untested in struggle — were assigned to such a delicate task as bank expropriations to obtain the required funds for the sharpening of the class struggle in the countryside.

During this whole stage, the putschist deviation of Pereyra, Martorell, Aragón, and other comrades, together with my syndicalist deviation, was leading us unconsciously, although no less perniciously, to neglect the great task: the formation and consolidation of the party, primarily on the basis of the mass work that had been developed.

My syndicalist deviation was by then so strong that I was incapable of directing assistance for the formation of the party in the countryside.

We consider that there is nothing more moral than to retrieve, for the people's liberation, the wealth stolen from them by the exploiters. Nevertheless, the expropriations that we carried out were premature, in that we did not have a solid party apparatus that would guarantee their effectiveness, and we had only untested militants, hastily recruited, to carry them out. Tasks of this nature can be successfully carried out only by comrades of iron, of a fully tested moral fiber.

After the expropriations, what we had anticipated actually happened: a fierce repression (jailings and persecution) against us that caused a general collapse — the Cuzco FIR, the national FIR, our expropriating apparatus, our military apparatus — everything, except for the one existing solid thing: the peasant movement. Although they could not jail me, thanks to the protection of the peasant movement, my activity was severely curtailed because of the repression.

After this disaster to the party, cells of the FIR began to function in Chaupimayo in a significant way. We also made efforts to establish such cells in other places, although with little success, due to my restricted mobility during the repression and to the lack of tested party cadres.

In Chaupimayo we set up a "general staff." It was an executive council that combined union and political tasks with those of a military character. This organization centralized the revolutionary work in the unions of La Convención and Lares, and of the whole department, through the delegates from the different unions, including those from Chaupimayo.

The rapid revolutionary polarization of the entire union tendency in Chaupimayo was very evident. Delegates from unions in other departments were beginning to join in. Unfortunately, even then the vanguard did not coalesce into an organization.

After a time, because of the great importance of the valley of Lares, we sent Comrade Blanca Labarrera there (she was new in the zone and in the party). Before long, she was taken prisoner, together with the entire leadership of that valley. Later on, the leadership was divided between Chaupimayo and the mobile guerrilla units.

4
Two Lines

In order to understand the methodologies of the principal tendencies in the Cuzco peasant movement, it is essential to understand that within the movement was repeated once again the confrontation, which has arisen and will continue to arise throughout the world, between Stalinism and its successors, on one hand, and Trotskyism, on the other. It is necessary to understand above all the reasons for this confrontation, the profound reasons that produce two distinct methodologies.

Stalinism arose in the Soviet Union as a political expression of the bureaucracy, of that excrescence (or *ch'upo,* as we say here) that issued from the triumphant but exhausted working class of the first workers' state; of that bureaucracy created by Russia's backwardness, by the exhaustion of the people, and the isolation of their revolution; of that bureaucracy stimulated by the vestiges of capitalism in the USSR, such as the rich peasants (kulaks).

That bureaucracy usurped power in the Soviet Union, making use of all the negative factors affecting the revolution. Although those factors were not strong enough to wipe out the great victory that the Bolshevik revolution meant for the world, the bureaucracy developed an increasingly reactionary policy by means of which it politically and physically liquidated the revolutionary leadership of October.

The bureaucracy, which was deforming the workers' state in its own interest, not only distorted Soviet foreign policy for the same purpose, but did much worse. Utilizing the prestige that the great proletarian revolution enjoyed among the world's Communist parties, it began subtly, in the name of that revolution to deform the Communist parties throughout the world, politically and organizationally, converting them from the national sections of a world revolutionary party, which they had been, into mere instruments of Soviet foreign policy, that is, the foreign policy of the bureaucracy.

The politics of the Soviet bureaucracy have not been, and are not now, the politics of the working class and its worldwide revolution; but neither have they been the politics of the bourgeoisie and imperialism and its worldwide counterrevolution.

The Soviet Union is a workers' state, degenerated in the interests of the bureaucracy; but it is a workers' state, not a capitalist state. The bureaucracy has warped social distribution for its own benefit, but the foundations of the economy continue to be socialist. The tremendously contradictory phenomenon that the bureaucracy of a workers' state represents also produces tremendously contradictory politics.

The bureaucracy is one of the fruits of the contradictions between capitalism and socialism; between proletarian revolution and bourgeois counterrevolution. As such, it has a transitory existence and lacks historical perspective; it is not even a class, but rather the pathological excrescence of a class.

It knows that the international triumph of socialism will sweep it away; it likewise knows that the triumph of the bourgeois counterrevolution would mean its destruction. To prolong its existence, therefore, it has to try to maintain the status quo, an equilibrium between proletarian revolution and bourgeois counterrevolution; meanwhile, it fights to increase its privileges within the context of that contradiction.

These considerations take their "theoretical" form in such theories as those of "socialism in one country" and "peaceful coexistence."

This defense of the existing equilibrium manifests itself in a contradictory, fluctuating policy that zigzags between left and right but in general follows a reactionary course. In general the bureaucracy adopts a reformist line in the capitalist countries which, while it may coincide with the line of other reformists, has a different origin.

The carrying out of such contradictory policies would of course require the existence of a monolithic organization, bureaucratized to the hilt. Such policies could not survive Bolshevik democratic centralism. The bureaucracy needed a pyramid of concrete with a Stalin at the top. After erecting just that kind of structure for its representative, the bureaucracy proceeded to deify him, fantastically falsifying history, making him appear the sole successor to Lenin. After his death Lenin's name was manipulated at will by the bureaucracy, which converted him into a defender of "socialism in one country," "peaceful coexistence," "revolution by stages," and whatever other "theories" it required for its ends. Stalin was at its top, steward of the revolution, faultless in his political vision, righteous liquidator of all the "agents of imperialism" (who, in Lenin's time and part of Stalin's era had been in the party leadership). Stalin was portrayed as an expert on the "socialist" arts and sciences, patron and favorite muse of socialist realism, infallible and irrefutable. Whoever disagreed with this personification of eternal truth was compelled either to undergo self-criticism or be condemned as an agent of imperialism — and at times both.

This bureaucratic monolith, an irreconcilable caricature of Marxism, could not last very long, for it had weak foundations. The death of Stalin was only the apparent cause of its crumbling. The advance of the anticapitalist revolution produced its effect on the monolith. The Soviet masses, protagonists and offspring of the October Revolution, were not going to support bureaucratic totalitarianism indefinitely.

The Chinese Revolution was a serious blow against monolithism. Then came the formidable Cuban Revolution. The Chinese Revolution was led by a Stalinized party against Stalin's opposition. The Cuban Revolution was led by Fidel and the July 26 Movement, which had nothing to do with the Cuban Communist Party.

The decline and fall of the Stalinist (and post-Stalinist) bureaucratic apparatus is hastened by the development of the worldwide socialist revolution; the workers of the workers' states are playing an important role in this process.

These were the politics that Trotskyism had to struggle against in Cuzco in order to impel the peasant struggle toward revolution; and this was at a time when the decline of Stalinism was not yet so far advanced. In that period, the Communist Party still considered itself the unchallenged proprietor of the Peruvian revolution (although it considered the revolution remote, as remote as possible). In that period, the Communist Party unhesitatingly defined Trotskyists as "agents of imperialism." (In Cuzco they added "and agents of the *gamonales*," as their local theoretical contribution.)

Here as elsewhere, Stalinism disguised its opportunism by dividing the revolutionary program into a minimum and a maximum program. In accordance with this, they put forth a series of aims "which can be achieved" within the present system; and in the remote future is the maximum program of power and socialism. As a result of this mechanical division, the reformist slogans of the minimum program aim at resolving the class conflicts *within* the present system. The class enemy, also interested in perpetuating this system, has similar aims. Their differences are in the terms of the solution: but it is not unusual for the two to coincide.

The central axis of Trotskyism, as is well known, is the Transitional Program which, as Comrade Pierre Frank explains in his brilliant article devoted to this subject, "formulates a political program aimed at mobilizing the masses into actions which correspond to their level of consciousness at a given moment, in order to lead them, through the education they receive in the course of these actions, to the highest level of consciousness, which will carry them to the conquest of power."[1]

So for us, as Rosa Luxemburg said, "socialism *is* the minimum we have to achieve these days." Each victory won is valuable to the extent that the fight for that victory educates the masses, giving them increasing understanding about the irreconcilability of the class struggle, the potentially invincible power they possess, and about the urgent necessity for the seizure of power and for socialism.

Therefore, we look for ways to win battles, not to "solve" conflicts, for the simple reason that there is only one solution: the socialist revolution.

It would be absurd to think that the classic Transitional Program written in 1938 provides answers to all the problems posed by a changing process of class struggle. It is precisely the task of the Fourth International to elaborate continually on the Transitional Program with the lessons learned in the struggle.

At times, certain transitional slogans are inappropriate for us to raise; or they are incorrect in the form or at the time that we raise them; but this does not invalidate the method — it is only an indication of the limits of the struggle. That was what happened more than once to us in Peru.

Precisely one of the aspects that requires the most theoretical elaboration is that relating to the peasantry in the poor countries. From the section of the 1938 Transitional Program dealing with the peasantry, one deduces that the reference is to the transitory victories of the peasantry in the advanced countries.

What we had in Cuzco, then, was a confrontation between the Transitional Program — inadequately applied and without a party, and for that reason mutilated — and the reformist minimum program. Fortunately, the general principles of Marxist methodology on waging the class struggle by means of the mobilization of masses are valid in any country and displayed in Cuzco once again their effectiveness in the successes achieved by the revolutionary developments in the countryside.

The program of the Communist Party for the peasantry of Cuzco, although it was never formally presented, can be summed up in the following points:

● To demand that in La Convención the Law of Yanaconaje on costs be applied, according to which the peasants would pay 20 percent of the crop to the landowner in settlement of rent.

● Collective claims on mountain lands. Something like the colonization plan for the *selva* put forward by the Peruvian right wing, a plan that consisted of transferring peasants from the sierra to the interior of a strange and inhospitable *selva,* which was lacking in roads and all means of communication, and all the services that they imply.

● To buy the land collectively from the landlords. That was the solution they proposed to the conflict of the Lauramarca peasants, who were kicked off their lands by a foreign-owned cattle-farming enterprise; they bought some of the lands, and of course this was not the best land by a long shot.

● To demand an agrarian reform law that would make a study of land expropriation. They will have no reason to grumble about the present law which does study expropriation with payment; for the Communist Party members clearly proposed either expropriation with payment or left the point obscure; our demand for confiscation of the land without payment vexed them.

The basic features of our program were the following:

● Unification of the lists of demands. The Communist Party members always rejected this, maintaining that "from one hacienda to another the demands are different." Some landowners submitted with difficulty, and there was no reason to put off settlements on their haciendas. It was also necessary to respect pacts that had originally been written by the unions, although because of the weakness of the organization in its early days, these were subsequently considered disadvantageous. It was much later, and with other perspectives, that we succeeded in winning the demand for a uniform list of demands.

● Basing the struggle primarily on mass mobilizations and regarding the court battles as secondary. On the other hand, the Communist Party members considered the mass mobilizations secondary. As is well known, mass mobilizations are very closely tied to the whole conception of the class struggle, of the formation of the elements and sectors of the vanguard.

If the court struggles are fundamental, it is more important to have a good staff of lawyers than mass organizations with appropriate leadership. It also follows from such an orientation that in electing leaders it is important to keep in mind primarily their level of literacy and knowledge of the laws.

And that is how the Communist Party did understand it.
Dr. Tupayachi stated that an organization of so many af-
filiates should be able to decide to erect a magnificent building
in the city of Cuzco to house the legal offices of the federation.

When a group of peasants asked the federation to send a commission to organize them, the different orientations became
clear: If members of the Communist Party were sent, they
recommended that the peasants elect those who were the most
well-read and who understood something about the law. As
is well known — because such people usually suffer less exploitation — they are generally the most conciliatory. If we
were sent, we recommended that the peasants elect those who
had demonstrated the most courage, the most interest in the
common problems, the most dynamism, regardless of whether
they knew how to read. Although at times we could not say
it in a clear and complete form, our argument in this respect
was: To call a strike you don't have to know how to read; to
organize a meeting you don't have to know how to read; to
handle a sling you don't have to know how to read; and
even to fire a gun it is not essential that you know how to
read.

The principal forms of mass mobilizations were meetings,
work stoppages, and strikes. It is not that the Stalinists plainly
rejected these forms of struggle, just as the Trotskyists did not
plainly reject courtroom proceedings. The difference is in the
degree of importance given the different forms of struggle.

Mass meetings took place principally in the city of Cuzco and
in Quillabamba, capital of the province of La Convención. The
peasant meetings acquired a much greater significance than any
others.

In Cuzco, for centuries, the Indian had slouched along the
streets with his *poncho* and his whispered Quechua; he had
never dared, even when drunk, to mount the sidewalk or speak
his Quechua out loud with his head held high. He was fearful
of the *misti* (the non-Indian), who was the master of the city.
He fled from the authorities or from whoever could force him
to do a job for a pittance — or for nothing; or who could force
him to sell his few products brought from the countryside at
any price offered him. The city of Cuzco meant all that to the
Indian, who was degraded and humiliated on the streets, the
plazas, in stores, markets, and public transportation. The city
meant more, too: courts of law, the offices of lawyers and
notaries public, the provincial jail, the landlord's residence,

where frequently a peasant, his wife, or his children had to do unpaid domestic work.

The mass meeting put the Indian on top of the monster. A concentration of *ponchos* in the main plaza, the heart of the city. At the court on the cathedral portico, which dominates the plaza like a rostrum. The odor of *coca* and Quechua, permeating the air. Quechua, out loud from the throat; Quechua shouted, threatening, tearing away the centuries of oppression. A march down the main streets, before and after the meeting. Windows and doors of the powerful fearfully slammed shut at the advance of the multitudes, aggressive, insulting, threatening, shouting in Quechua truths silenced by centuries of Castilian Spanish. The Indian, master of plazas and streets, of the entire street and the sidewalk. That's what the peasant meetings meant, aside from the specific object for each gathering.

The twenty-four- or forty-eight-hour work stoppages in the countryside also had a significance distinct from those in the city. The paralysis of agricultural work just for those periods did not have any effect. The tenant farmer is obliged to work a specified number of days each month for the landlord; normally there are days when he is absent without this affecting the fulfillment of his obligation. The only one to suffer by a one- or two-day work stoppage on the land would have been the peasant, since for the most part it would have stopped work only on his own fields.

In view of this, the peasant work stoppage was a stoppage of transportation, of industrial and commercial activities, etc., throughout the province; a total paralysis imposed by the peasantry organized in picket lines. Logically, this also meant a total paralysis of agricultural work, but the main reason for this was that the peasants were engaged in activities in zones that were distant from their homes.

It was on these occasions that the peasants felt their own power most forcefully. Even the office of the sub-prefect, the highest political authority in the province, had to shut down. Even personal travel from one place to another was carried out only with the permission of the peasants.

The strikes of the peasants also have a content distinct from the urban strikes. The urban strike, although it hurts the employer, also means a sacrifice by the workers. Generally, if it is not widened, the longer it lasts, the weaker it tends to become.

Work for the landlord on the part of the peasants, tenant

farmers, etc., discharges the obligation to pay rent for the parcels of land the peasants work for themselves. This means that the strike (which, to make itself felt, must last at least a month) affects only the landlord and benefits the peasants, giving them free time for work on their own land. If there is anything that hurts the strikers, it will be the repression against the strike, not the strike itself; logically, the Trotskyists had to fight with the utmost effort to maintain the principle that the whole union that went on strike had to refuse to make up the unworked days after the strike, because, if this principle had been broken, the advantages of the strike would have disappeared and it would have become converted into a liability for the peasants.

Another important form of mobilization was on the issue of evicted peasants. The key case was that of Vega Caboy, a nonunionized tenant on the Aranjuez hacienda.

The landlord, Dalmiro Casafranca, had initiated the customary lawsuit to evict him in order to take possession of his fields. As usual, the landlord won in the courts of Cuzco and in the Supreme Court. Vega came to the provincial federation when he had been told of the judgement against him. According to law, he had no further option; he had to abandon the "leased" land.

The position of the Communist Party bureaucracy was that this was a lesson for the peasants not to hire Aprista lawyers, as Vega had done, but federation lawyers. According to them, at this stage of affairs, in the light of the Supreme Court decision, there was nothing to be done.

Our position was that the judgement had been negative because of the class character of the courts, which are no more than instruments of the exploiters. The organization of the peasantry would have to use its own strength against this decision, building a gigantic gathering on Vega Caboy's farm the day his eviction was to be finalized. We said:

> This is the first kernel of a ton of maize that they would like to thresh; if we permit them this kernel, it will be very easy for them to get all the rest. There are several judgements of this type pending against union leaders; lawsuits opened for the purpose of reprisal. If the enemy courts see that we are indifferent in this case, they will be encouraged to rule against us in others; the leaders will be evicted, the fear among the peasantry will spread, the *gamonales* will initiate new lawsuits. On the other hand, if we dem-

onstrate our firm opposition in this case and any other
that arises, they will refrain from ordering evictions precisely to maintain the prestige of the law and the courts.
And the *gamonales* will find themselves forced to abandon
this form of repression.

We issued a fairly good resolution — good enough to fright-
en the functionaries whose task it was to carry out the eviction,
so that they all began to decline the job under various excus-
es. For the first time in a case like this the *gamonal* was heard
muttering, "There is no justice for me!" The eviction was called
off.

In this case, the mere threat of a mobilization was enough;
in previous cases, small mobilizations were sufficient to prevent evictions; the authorities knew that behind those token
delegations stood thousands of peasants equally ready to step
forward.

The most widely known cases were the mobilization at
Pachachaca Grande under the command of Comrade Aniceto
Muñoz, the future guerrilla, and the mobilizations of Chaupimayo. Our union agreed that anyone who had an eviction
case pending should disregard the court order and should
use the money saved up for the lawsuit to buy a gun instead —
"to change lawyers," as it was put by Comrade Andrés Gonzales, who was himself the first to make this change.

Besides the pressure put on the courts by the mass mobilizations, there were several occasions on which the masses
actually freed prisoners. Chaupimayo by itself freed Comrade
Fortunato Vargas on one occasion and me on another; these
actions came as a consequence of night marches by the union
members en masse to the police station where Vargas was
held prisoner, in the first instance, and, in the other, to the
highway, where they stopped and searched all passing vehicles
including the one in which I was being transported.

Throughout all the developments, we explained to the peasants that we would get our hands on the land only through
our own power; and that we had to confront the enemy with
arms, until we could destroy the government of the exploiters
and replace it with a government of workers and peasants.
The CP, of course, said nothing about this, but requested an
agrarian reform law, and groveled at the doors of legislators
who were "on the side of the workers" in the hope that they
would grant such a law.

When we realized that a prolonged strike would, in actuality, shatter the system of property relations in the zone, we sought to make a long-term and general strike. With this aim, we gave a new and powerful impulse to our old project for a uniform list of demands; but this time with the understanding that rejection of these demands would be the signal for a long-term general strike.

The set of demands we put forth had no likelihood of acceptance. We ignored strictly legal considerations; we took into account the ridiculously low price that the *gamonales* had paid for the mountain lands (I think it was ten cents per hectare [one hectare = 2.5 acres]). Since the landowners had contributed absolutely nothing to the improvement of the lands leased to the peasants, which consisted of tracts of virgin semi-*selva*; and since the construction of roads had also cost them nothing, the price we offered to pay them was virtually a gift. (If I remember correctly, twenty to forty Peruvian dollars rent a year per hectare, varying with the productivity of the land.)

It is true that within the framework of bourgeois legalities, the price we were offering was, according to this reasoning, too high. Nevertheless, it was guaranteed to give any *gamonal* a heart attack and was unacceptable to the government.

Along with this, we called for a full-scale fund-raising campaign to launch a gigantic publicity campaign throughout the country in favor of our proposal — publicity that would have helped us in spreading the movement.

At first our project, taking the Communist Party by surprise, won out. I was even named as one of the members of the commission that was to go to Lima. However, the CP could not go along with so much; it was a huge step forward toward the revolution. The Stalinist bureaucracy mobilized itself to the utmost: the leaders of the FTC, the legal counselors, and even some student elements turned La Convención inside out to prevent both the passage of that unified list of demands and my participation in the commission.

They said the same as always: the Trotskyists were proposing an unacceptable unified set of demands and a campaign on a national scale as a provocation in the service of the *gamonales* and the imperialists; and it was inconceivable that Hugo Blanco, "the well-known international provocateur in the service of imperialism," should be allowed to stay in the federation.

The lack of an organized Trotskyist party once again made itself felt. The original agreement was withdrawn to make way for an "acceptable" list of demands; the commission membership was changed to make it suitable for carrying out the transactions by bureaucratic means and without mass mobilizations. The lawyers generously offered to work for free on elaborating and processing the demands and asserted that the massive fund-raising campaign that had been projected was therefore unnecessary.

And so the uniform list began to travel the bureaucratic route that reformism esteems so highly; as a springboard for a general strike and a means of extending the movement, it was discarded.

Nevertheless, the peasantry was daily becoming more combative, and we were only waiting for a favorable occasion to directly propose the general strike; unfortunately, the problem of publicizing and spreading the movement was much more difficult.

The occasion presented itself with the massacre of twenty-two peasants in Pasco. Under the pressure of Lucho Zapata (a hero of the Peruvian revolution who participated in the Javier Heraud guerrilla band of the ELN [National Liberation Army] in 1965), and other members of the FIR, the FTC held a meeting in Cuzco and raised three demands: the return to the Pasco peasants of the lands which were in the hands of the Cerro de Pasco Copper Corporation (a Yankee enterprise that had been encroaching on communal lands in various departments in the center of the country); the punishment of the Civil Guards who had committed the murders; and compensation for the families of the murdered peasants.

We used those same points in calling a long-term general strike in the valleys of La Convención and Lares. The assembly of the provincial federation endorsed the strike. The local bureaucrats were disoriented by the points on which we based the strike call. They were the same points that the departmental hierarchy had accepted without much objection as the demands of the meeting. Logically it might be one thing to raise them as demands in a meeting, but it was quite another to make them the grounds for a general strike.

The general strike was successfully carried out for two months by the peasants of the valleys. We understood its profound significance as a crack in the existing property system, and we knew that the government would ultimately be forced to conduct an armed repression. We explained this to the peasants, pointing out to them the urgency of preparing for armed resistance to the attack.

The CP utilized the situation to call for lifting the strike in view of the danger of repression. Their motion passed. Nevertheless, we were able to carry a motion supporting the principle we had defended in the strikes of individual unions, namely, that the strike would be called off only on those haciendas that agreed to recognize the two months of strike as time worked (that is, not to be made up). Many haciendas refused to accept this, and the strikes there continued. Of course, the strike also went on in the cases of those unions that were striking because of their own particular grievances.

Much later, when I was already imprisoned, a general strike was called again, at the time that the government abolished the statute that was the basis for the 1962 agrarian reform law. That strike has continued to the present. It is unquestionable that the reason it has not been suppressed is the authorities' fear that the armed struggle, which emerged in embryonic form in La Convención, might be transformed into a mass struggle.

Until now the government has in general accepted this situation as fact, choosing to find a way out through the agrarian reform laws that purport to legalize the possession of leased and subleased lands by the peasants, on the condition that they agree to pay for those lands in installments. Up to the present time, the peasants of La Convención and Lares have for the most part refused to pay; and on this question, the resolutions of their last congress are emphatic.

The fate of the peasants of La Convención and of the entire department will be the fate of the Peruvian peasantry as a whole.

I shall take up matters related to the armed struggle in the next chapter.

5
Dual Power

In view of the ignorance or erroneous interpretation of our concept of dual power, even among those on the left, we felt obliged to transcribe some paragraphs by Trotsky on this subject. To the question, What constitutes the essence of dual power? Trotsky answers:

> Antagonistic classes exist in society everywhere, and a class deprived of power inevitably strives to some extent to swerve the governmental course in its favor. This does not as yet mean, however, that two or more powers are ruling in society. The character of a political structure is directly determined by the relation of the oppressed classes to the ruling class. A single government, the necessary condition of stability in any regime, is preserved so long as the ruling class succeeds in putting over its economic and political forms upon the whole of society as the only forms possible.[1]

Trotsky affirms that the coexistence of power does not always imply duality of power. He cites the case of the landholding nobility and the bourgeoisie in Prussia; we can cite the case of the *gamonales* and the bourgeoisie in Peru, in that "no matter how sharp at times may be the conflict between the two participating powers, they have a common social basis. Therefore their clash does not threaten to split the state apparatus. The two-power regime arises only out of irreconcilable class conflicts — is possible, therefore, only in a revolutionary epoch, and constitutes one of its fundamental elements."

He continues:

> The political mechanism of revolution consists of the transfer of power from one class to another. The forcible overturn is usually accomplished in a brief time. But no

historic class lifts itself from a subject position to a position of rulership suddenly in one night, even though a night of revolution. It must already on the eve of the revolution have assumed a very independent attitude towards the official ruling class; moreover, it must have focussed upon itself the hopes of intermediate classes and layers, dissatisfied with the existing state of affairs, but not capable of playing an independent role. The historic preparation of a revolution brings about, in the prerevolutionary period, a situation in which the class which is called to realize the new social system, although not yet master of the country, has actually concentrated in its hands a significant share of the state power, while the official apparatus of the government is still in the hands of the old lords. That is the initial dual power in every revolution.

Farther on:

This double sovereignty does not presuppose — generally speaking, indeed, it excludes — the possibility of a division of the power into two equal halves, or indeed any formal equilibrium of forces whatever. It is not a constitutional, but a revolutionary fact. It implies that a destruction of the social equilibrium has already split the state superstructure. It arises where the hostile classes are already each relying upon essentially incompatible governmental organizations — the one outlived, the other in process of formation — which jostle against each other at every step in the sphere of government. The amount of power which falls to each of these struggling classes in such a situation, is determined by the correlation of forces in the course of the struggle.

In another paragraph, he indicates that although the participants make efforts to maintain the duality of power . . . "this system will nevertheless inevitably explode. Civil war gives to this double sovereignty its most visible, because territorial, expression. Each of the powers, having created its own fortified drill ground, fights for possession of the rest of the territory, which often has to endure the double sovereignty in the form of successive invasions by the two fighting powers, until one of them decisively installs itself."

For examples of dual power, Trotsky cites the English Revolution of the seventeenth century, the Great French Revolution, and the Paris Commune. In referring to the process of the Russian Revolution, he points to two cases of dual power:

> The Russian bourgeoisie, fighting with and coöperating with the Rasputin bureaucracy, had enormously strengthened its political position during the war. Exploiting the defeat of tzarism, it had concentrated in its hands, by means of the Country and Town unions and the Military-Industrial Committees, a great power. It had at its independent disposition enormous state resources, and was in the essence of the matter a parallel government. During the war the tzar's ministers complained that Prince Lvov was furnishing supplies to the army, feeding it, medicating it, even establishing barber shops for the soldiers. 'We must either put an end to this, or give the whole power into his hands,' said Minister Krivoshein in 1915. He never imagined that a year and a half later Lvov would receive 'the whole power' — only not from the tzar, but from the hands of Kerensky, Cheidze and Sukhanov. But on the second day after he received it, there began a new double sovereignty: alongside of yesterday's liberal half-government — today formally legalized — there arose an unofficial, but so much the more actual government of the toiling masses in the form of the soviets. From that moment the Russian revolution began to grow up into an event of world-historic significance.

Then Trotsky goes on to a more detailed explication of the phenomenon in the Russian Revolution, and to conclude the chapter on this theme, after some mention of Germany, he resumes the discussion in a general theoretical way.

> Does this phenomenon of the dual power — heretofore not sufficiently appreciated — contradict the Marxian theory of the state, which regards government as an executive committee of the ruling class? This is just the same as asking: Does the fluctuation of prices under the influence of supply and demand contradict the labor theory of value? Does the self-sacrifice of a female protecting her offspring refute the theory of a struggle for existence? No, in these phenomena we have a more complicated combination of the same laws. If the state is an organization of class rule, and a revolution is the overthrow of the ruling class, then the transfer of power from the one class to the other must necessarily create self-contradictory state

conditions, and first of all in the form of the dual power. The relation of class forces is not a mathematical quantity permitting *a priori* computations. When the old régime is thrown out of equilibrium, a new correlation of forces can be established only as the result of a trial by battle. That is revolution.

It may seem as though this theoretical inquiry has led us away from the events of 1917. In reality it leads right into the heart of them. It was precisely around this problem of twofold power that the dramatic struggle of parties and classes turned. Only from a theoretical height is it possible to observe it fully and correctly understand it.

Knowing what Trotsky said, anyone who suggests that we use "the dual power *method*," must be presumed to have dishonest intentions. We have never understood dual power as a method but as a *state of affairs,* a condition that arises in the course of the class struggle. It arises and occurs in all revolutionary processes; it occurred in China, in Cuba, and now in Vietnam (at present it is even demonstrated formally by the two hostile governments in South Vietnam). It is not therefore a method but a condition.

Another falsehood[2] is that we try to achieve dual power. Neither we nor the enemy try for this. The ruling class wants to be the only power, and the revolutionaries seek to destroy that power totally, to replace it with the workers' power.

It is too ironic a slander to attribute any theory of peaceful coexistence to Trotskyism, which of all groups has been the one to fight any form of that concept intransigently and to the death. If it is inconceivable on an international scale, it would be simply stupid to call for it on a local scale. If we do not believe in socialism in one country, we certainly do not believe in socialism in one province, or anything of that kind.

It is also a slander to claim that we look forward to or even consider the possibility of stabilizing that situation. As Trotsky's chapter on dual power points out: *"By its very nature, such a state of affairs cannot be stable. . . . This system will nevertheless inevitably explode."*

Many of our hastily arrived at positions regarding La Convención and Cuzco, taken without adequate preparation, had their origin precisely in our completely clear understanding that "this state of affairs cannot last." The bank expropriations were not designed to "stabilize" the situation, but to buy arms for the revolution. In July or August of 1962, I wrote to the comrades, showing them that this situation would not last more than six months. Why did we turn to guerrilla warfare without sufficient preparation? Precisely for that reason! Because we knew that the moment had arrived in which, if we did not make a decisive move, they would fall upon Chaupimayo and crush us.

It is certain that in Peru the duality of power on a national scale will not occur between bourgeois power and the peasantry, but between bourgeois power and the proletariat, in which are concentrated "the hopes of intermediate classes and layers, dissatisfied with the existing state of affairs, but not capable of playing an independent rôle."

But this does not contradict the local development, within this process, the development of incipient forms of dual power between the bourgeois government and sectors of the population other than the proletariat, which is practically nonexistent in many zones. It is within this context that we speak of the rise of dual power in La Convención and Cuzco.

In the countryside, the power acquired by the workers against the power of the exploiters has a clearer, more formal aspect than in the city.

It is necessary to remember the semifeudal features of the hacienda: the *gamonal* is not only the boss and owner of the means of production; he is the one who almost directly appoints judges and local officials, just as he appoints schoolteachers or closes schools. In large measure, he also supplants the local authorities in his functions: he enforces law and order directly. He can shut down shops (commercial establishments) or monopolize them.

To sum it up, he is almost a feudal lord. The power is clearly concentrated in him, unlike the situation in the cities where — although the power is still in the hands of the exploiters — the system is more complex, the transmission belts more hidden and disguised.

Under those circumstances, when the peasants have succeeded in organizing themselves to fight for better working conditions, they have in fact also succeeded in displacing the rule of the landowner in other respects.

It is not even necessary to tell organized peasants that when they have disputes among themselves they must not run to the common enemy in search of justice. The bias of the local authorities is so obvious that they too are gradually deprived of their functions.

Communal decision-making is reborn or strengthened in

all respects: local justice, public works, education, health, commerce. Mutual aid in agriculture is also strengthened.

We have previously said that "one of the reasons [for the rise of the peasant unions as an organ of power] is that the peasants work and live inside the same geographical unit, the scene of its members' activity. This is a fundamental characteristic of the peasant unions that differentiates them from the industrial trade unions.

"The peasants of a union are united not only by the *gamonal's* direct exploitation or direct abuse, but also by many common needs, such as the struggle against the exploitation, abuses, and biases of the authorities; for construction and improvement of roads, canals, fences; for the improvement of the production systems; against disease."

In reality, the peasants of the hacienda form a community (in the general sense of the word, not in the restricted Peruvian sense of an *ayllu*); that community has moved from being governed almost absolutely by the landlord to being governed collectively — that is, to peasant democracy.

It is understood that this process has not been completed, that it is a process that will be completed only with the revolution; but in every respect, even the formation of a peasant union is an enormous step forward.

From its birth, the peasant organization has a deeper, more extensive, more political significance than the workers' trade union.

We have spoken of the hacienda union. In the communal village or *ayllu,* the process is more complex because theoretically the communal village has certain democratic rights that in practice are more or less unrealized. At times the communal organism is so damaged that it is necessary to create another organization that will be the vehicle for the class struggle (E. Ongoy). At other times the communal organism itself is converted into the instrument of struggle (Pasco).

We cite some features of situations where the peasantry has achieved power, in Chaupimayo and elsewhere. In Chaupimayo we made ourselves owners of the land:

● The peasants retained ownership of the plots they cultivated for their own use and for which they had been obliged to pay rent in uncompensated labor for the landlord.

● The landlord's fields and buildings became the collective property of the union.

● The distribution of uncultivated land to everyone who wanted to till it was begun.

These measures spread wholly or in part to other unions and were formalized or encouraged by the agrarian reform

law that from my hiding place I issued in my capacity as
secretary of agrarian reform of the Departmental Peasants
Federation of Cuzco.

We formally named judges to replace the bourgeois authorities (their decisions were subject to appeal before the General
Assembly).

The police came very rarely, but communicated with the
union with proper advance notice, for example: "We have an
order to arrest so-and-so, we are going to come on such and
such a day; to spare us embarrassment, kindly see that on
that day the above-named persons are not home."

It should be understood that they did this out of fear that
we would attack them, and we did not attack them because
we still were not strong enough to take the consequences.

When a peasant who was not a member of the union lodged
a complaint against someone from Chaupimayo with the Civil
Guard of the district, they would tell him to go to the union
in search of justice, or to return to the Civil Guard barracks
with an order signed by our union authorizing them to attend
to the matter.

We built our schools ourselves and paid the teachers hired
by us and certified by the Ministry of Education. Public works
were in the hands of the union, which determined their priority.

All of this, of course, was backed by an embryonic armed
force, the developing peasant militia.

The rising level of consciousness

Because we were Trotskyists, we had no difficulty understanding that a process of dual power was unfolding and that
it was our duty to make the masses conscious of it. We used
each step, each successful advance, to the maximum as in-
struction, as a lesson, as a factor in educating the masses
and in raising their consciousness of their own power.

Thus we never wearied of explaining that the popular assemblies were our parliament, counterposed to the bourgeois
parliament, in whose election the peasants had not even participated, since the great majority were illiterate, and consequently could not vote.

We explained, of course, that the authority of the laws passed
by our "parliament" was maintained only by the power that
we had, not by their "legality." We explained that we had in
reality passed a law against the evictions, and that we were
quite capable of making it stick.

In the work stoppages (the peasant work stoppage meant
paralyzing transportation, commercial and industrial activities,

and so forth, in the entire province) and in the meetings, the peasants' power was made more evident, and we explained then that the strike call was a paralyzing decree issued by the peasantry, and that if it succeeded it was because we had the strength to enforce it, no matter how illegal it was declared by the bourgeois power.

On one occasion, during a work stoppage, a merchant wanted to leave Quillabamba. A peasant picket line blocked his way, informing him that he would need a pass signed by the appropriate authority. The merchant returned with a pass signed by the sub-prefect. The peasant strikers then explained to him that the appropriate authority during work stoppages was not the sub-prefect, nor any bourgeois authority, but the strike council elected by the peasants. Choking back his rage, the merchant had to come soliciting my signature as president of the strike council. Although travel by foot had not been prohibited, the pickets had taken that position to humiliate this powerful merchant who had such a special hatred for us.

As the process advanced, we made each demonstration of peasant power more formal and more explicit.

The military junta in 1962 prohibited throughout Peru both the military and the student parades that took place each year during the national celebration (July 28, Independence Day). In Chaupimayo we carried off both ceremonies with all the formalities of the occasion, explaining in speeches on the subject that in reality the army marching on that date was the only true Peruvian army and that although our Union Defense Brigade was very weak, it constituted the embryo of what would become in the future the people's army, the army of workers and peasants, the authentic Peruvian army.

Domestic justice, which had previously been administered by the secretary of order, passed into the hands of specially named judges (whose decisions, to be sure, continued to be subject to appeal before the assembly).

In the night school that functioned during the final stage in Chaupimayo, and which (unlike the day school) had nothing to do with the official curriculum, it was explained in the course on civic education:

> *Chambers* (*of Deputies and Senators*) — conglomeration of servants of the *gamonales* and capitalists appointed by them to pass laws to maintain the exploitation of the poor by the rich.
> *Civil Guard* — armed organization whose purpose is to commit outrages against the people for the benefit of the rich.

> *Secretary of Defense* — minister of war of the peasant union, entrusted with every aspect of its defense, in accord with its strength, from legal defense within bourgeois laws to armed defense and struggle to seize power for the workers and peasants.

In this vein ran all the courses in civics, history, and so forth.

Also dating from this period are the decrees that we issued (the agrarian reform law and others), and those that were important were issued with all requisite formality.

All these means of instilling in the masses a consciousness of the irreconcilable antagonisms between classes, between exploiters and exploited, have met with the strangest criticisms. It is said that our decrees are a sign that we overestimated our forces; this criticism comes from a failure to understand that they were instruments for raising consciousness, and that in practice they extended the struggle. (Encouraged by the agrarian reform law that we distributed in leaflet form, peasants in other zones began to seize the land.)

The same critics accuse us of having tried to coexist with the bourgeois regime. However much we demonstrated, reiterated, raised consciousness, formalized the mortal antagonism between the classes, we did so only to . . . "coexist" [!].

The dual power that developed in La Convención and Lares and in other parts of the department of Cuzco was sharpest in Chaupimayo, Santa Rosa (after the decline of the Aprietas), and Paltaybamba (after it broke away from the union led by Herrera, a pro-landlord Stalinist). There the landlord was ordered to hand over his keys and disappear into another zone; it behooved him to obey, leaving his house and estate, his cultivated fields and the industrial installations in the hands of the union, which socialized them and used them collectively.

In that zone, the ancient chains could be heard snapping as they were cast off. The air became pure, collective, breathable. The water, the land, and the plants attained their true dimensions, a profound forecast of human accomplishment.

In the unity of the Assembly, the idea of rulers and ruled vanished, for there the judgements of the lowliest shaped decisions of gigantic import, the thought of each individual appeared as an inseparable particle of a single, great, powerful, collective mind. We are convinced that that was dual power.

6

The Question of
Armed Struggle and Putschism

In the revolution's bleakest periods, in the face of Stalinism and other types of reformist opportunism, the Trotskyists have had to defend the Marxist-Leninist concept that there is no possibility of the exploiters giving up power without a struggle. A peaceful transition to socialism is not possible; the armed struggle of the oppressed against the oppressors is an inevitable phase of the revolution.

In the most recent stage, we have had to combat the ultraleftists, for whom revolution is synonymous with guerrilla warfare carried on from one or more *focos*.[1] In Peru, several Fidelista groups have sprung up, and the Maoists combine this position with Stalinist opportunism.

We Trotskyists know that armed struggle is a necessary phase of the revolution, but it is only that — a phase. The revolutionary struggle is a process through which the masses rise in their organizational level, in their consciousness, in their forms of struggle, guided by their conscious vanguard, by the revolutionary party.

The masses naturally prefer to settle accounts peacefully. In the course of the process, they begin to realize that the exploiters will not step down and that they will respond to their demands only with violence; only then do the masses see the need of meeting the violence of the oppressors with their own violence. With the sharpening of this clash between the violence of the exploiters and the answering violence of the exploited, armed struggle arises inevitably.

We are not able to predict what form that armed struggle will take, or at what moment it will begin. In Russia, the civil war began after the seizure of power, and its main form was not guerrilla warfare. In Cuba, the armed struggle came first, led also by a party, but without combat organizations among the masses. It began in the form of guerrilla warfare carried out from a *foco*.

Nevertheless, in both instances it developed after *the masses* had come to see that armed struggle was the only solution.

I emphasize the role of the masses because that is the part the ultralefts do not understand; they believe that what is necessary is for *us,* the revolutionaries, to understand that the revolution will have to employ violence.

In Cuba, it was Batista who convinced the masses with his brutal tyranny that no legal recourse remained open to them. When the guerrilla *foco* arose, the people understood that it was the only road to their liberation.

In countries like Peru, the masses still have access to a wide range of activities other than military. When the masses push these activities to their ultimate conclusion, the government will find itself obliged to cast off its legalistic mask and openly employ violence in defense of the system of exploitation. Only then will the masses understand that there is no alternative to armed struggle.

If Comrade Fidel Castro, the guerrilla par excellence, believes it possible that in Peru socialism will come about without destroying the present government by force of arms, how can the Peruvian Fidelistas imagine that the masses, with their low political level, have already despaired of settling accounts by means that do not entail violence?

It is necessary to take into account that when we refer to means that do not entail violence, we do not mean only legal means, but also "illegal" mobilizations that the enemy still permits, that he still does not repress with violence. Such is the case of the factory workers who call an illegal strike; even if this isolated strike is suppressed, the workers still have not had extensive experience with strikes. While winning concessions by these means still seems possible to them, they will not choose armed struggle. That is the case with the peasants of La Convención at present, and of some communal villages of the sierra which won land through "illegal" mass mobilizations which the government was afraid to attack with armed violence precisely for fear of the reaction. It is simpleminded to think that those people are going to choose armed struggle unless they feel forced into it by circumstances.

It is very possible that rural guerrilla warfare will be one form of armed struggle in Peru; but we cannot say that it will be the chief form. It seems to us that the more widespread and uniform the movement, the less spontaneous it is, the greater will be the importance of the relatively stable militias, both urban and rural.

In our case, it was precisely the isolation that obliged us to convert from a militia to a guerrilla band.

It is also necessary to explain that we are not against guer-

rilla warfare in principle, but we are certainly against using
it artificially, out of context. We believe that guerrilla bands
will arise fundamentally as ours did, that is, as a result of
the political development of the local peasants. If our work
is integrated into the development of mass political consciousness, there is no reason to turn to artificial guerrilla activity;
it appears to us that if we need to use such activity, it will
be as an exception, not the rule.

In summary, for us, the Trotskyists, guerrilla warfare is a
tactic that may be used in a particular country under particular conditions, but it is not a strategy.

Militias in La Convención and Lares

In La Convención, once the union organizing was somewhat
advanced, we began propaganda about armed struggle, at
first among the vanguard and then cautiously, but gradually,
among the masses in a broad but informal way. For this
purpose, we made use of the memory of the *montoneros,*
groups of armed civilians used in the last century and at the
beginning of this century by some local despots in the struggles
among themselves. Often the landlords would draft the peasants into their service as *montoneros.* This memory survives
among the peasants. We would comment that, if necessary,
the peasants would have to use *montoneros* in their own defense. Later, after the Cuban peasantry had won the land,
the mere mention of the Cuban example served us as propaganda for armed struggle. (On one occasion, the Stalinists
tried to expel me from the FTC for this propaganda. The
maneuver backfired; the debate served as further propaganda
for armed struggle.)

Some peasants in the vanguard began to acquire arms,
declaring that a weapon was the best lawyer. In Chaupimayo,
we began to institute informal target practice for women as
well as men. As it was not the custom for women to hunt,
the mere photograph of a peasant woman from the zone with
a carbine in her hand raised the spirits of the peasants in
other unions.

One of the work stoppages served us well by raising peasant consciousness about armed struggle. The zone of Huiro
was assigned to the Chaupimayo union. (I was not with them
because I was then serving as president of the strike committee in Quillabamba.) Chaupimayo behaved in Huiro with
its customary energy. The fury of one of the *gamonales* led
him to set out armed to attack the peasants; after evading

the landowner's attack, they decided to relieve him of his weapon. After the Chaupimayo people returned to their own locale, another incident occurred, this time with a policeman in the town of Santa María. The result was identical — the peasants took away the weapon.

Their return was ecstatic, triumphal; the secretary of the women's front, a militant comrade, walked around with the policeman's cap on her head and his rifle slung over her shoulder.

When I was reunited with my comrades after returning from Quillabamba, we took advantage of these incidents to call an educational assembly. We pointed out their symbolic character: "This is what the Peruvian people will do in the future — seize the weapons from the hands of the oppressors and their servants — that will be the principal way of arming ourselves."

The strength and pressure of the Stalinists in the federation obliged us to return the weapon to the police, to avoid a severe repression. We have still not returned the weapon of the *gamonal.*

In any case, these symbolic events helped us propagandize for armed struggle.

When the class contradictions sharpened, we began in Chaupimayo to initiate formal guerrilla training with the assistance of vanguard elements from other unions. The militia in Chaupimayo arose, although at first we avoided giving it a formal character because of the Stalinist opposition, which was based on the low level of the other unions.

The FIR raised the question of getting the provincial federation's formal approval for the organization of the Union Defense Brigade. We tried to have this demand approved, explaining its necessity because of the general strike. However, we were defeated; the Stalinists succeeded in getting approval for calling off the strike.

Subsequently, in view of the combativeness of the peasants of Lares, the landowners in the region began to carry arms and threaten the peasants. (Among other things, there were two unsuccessful attempts on my life while I was on an organizing trip through the zone.) The peasants of Lares protested before the provincial federation, which told them to take their problems to the police; we waited patiently for the peasants to go through this experience, certain that the results would provide an even better foundation for our demands. The peasants of Lares returned indignantly to the federation, reporting that the police had told them that the landowners were right and prudent to bear arms, and to shoot the peasants in self-defense. Appeals to other authorities had similar results.

That was what we had expected would happen. We explained that if the landowners were armed and threatening the peasants and if the police, also armed, were clearly on the side of the landowners, the only recourse was for the peasants to arm themselves.

The Stalinists were on the defensive; they claimed there was a danger that the comrades would make improper and irresponsible use of their weapons — when they got drunk, for example. We answered that they were perfectly correct, that such a danger did actually exist. It was precisely for that reason that the federation should approve the organization of disciplined Union Defense Brigades to be in charge of training practice.

The Stalinists had to keep silent, the delegates of Lares and La Convención overwhelmingly approved this motion and named two people to be in charge of this work for the federation: I was one of them.

By this time, the intelligence police were trying to capture me, though without much enthusiasm. After my assignment by the federation, the likelihood of my capture increased, and I had to be more careful.

With that resolution we were authorized to extend the organization and preparation of militias. It was an official resolution of the federation, which, although it had no legal standing with the authorities, certainly had such standing with the peasants, who very much respected their federation.

Unfortunately, we could not take maximum advantage of this great breakthrough because of the sorry lack of a party. Shortly thereafter, a severe repression was instituted against the FIR for the bank expropriations.

I took refuge in the mountains, with the rearguard, protected by the peasants. Together with Pedro Candela, a fugitive from one of the expropriations, and another FIR comrade from the city, who was just getting used to peasant work, we began mountain life, making use of the opportunity to adapt ourselves to the guerrilla life.

Then, gradually, taking all appropriate security measures, I began to moderate my isolation. I left the mountain to return to the peasant zone and continue my work.

The disadvantage of having to remain in the most secure zone forced an isolated intensification of the work in Chaupimayo. For the most part, I organized party cells and intensified the preparation of the militia in Chaupimayo and neighboring unions.

Another measure adopted by the union dating from this period was the posting of armed sentinels. This work was carried out by groups of union members, in rotation. During the day this was unnecessary, for the families that lived on the outskirts had had the prudence to post sentinels. And so the union avoided being taken by surprise.

Since I was the most persecuted, I had to take additional security measures, among them sleeping each night in a different house or farm, or on the mountain, always with my guerrilla equipment at hand. Other comrades who were also persecuted took similar precautions.

The Stalinists, aided by the repression, developed great strength in the federation; this, plus our lack of a party and the repression itself, produced the accentuated polarization of the vanguard around Chaupimayo. "There is another federation!" protested the CP bureaucrats who were pastured in Quillabamba.

In Chaupimayo, intensive training was carried out with the participation of other comrades who came sporadically, not only from La Convención and Lares, but from other parts of the department of Cuzco. Instructors were also sent to other vanguard unions in La Convención and Lares.

The sporadic actions of the Chaupimayo militias had begun even before the federation had officially approved the formation of the brigades. In Chaupimayo and other unions, besides serving as standby defense for the peasants and increasing their self-confidence, the militias performed the functions of expelling traitors from the zone, confiscating for the benefit of the union the profits of the cruellest landlords, organizing peasants in the zones with the greatest *gamonal* strength, and expelling landlords.

Also in Lares, during the period of the greatest expansion of the peasant movement, the peasants disarmed two policemen; and some landlords appeared at the district federation assembly (which had already been organized) to hand over their weapons "for the revolution." They were told that if they were with the revolution they should issue a public statement announcing that the peasants were carrying out the agrarian reform correctly, that there was social peace, that they earnestly requested the government not to disturb the tranquility of the zone. The landowners made that public declaration, which was circulated in leaflet form. Of course, nobody believed that the landlords were "with the revolution," but it was one important way of dividing the enemy. Similar events took place in the zone of La Joya in La Convención under the leadership of the great Benito Cutipa. This was the peak of the peasant upsurge, with various *gamonales* expelled from the zone and their wealth confiscated by the peasants.

Nevertheless, the peasant movement of La Convención and Lares was isolated — even from the rest of the department which was its rearguard. Moreover, we could not rely on even a minimal party apparatus in the zone. The union leadership, for all its breadth and complexity, even in its best moments could not substitute for that.

Because of the lack of a party or other organization that could at least substitute for it in this work, the organization of the militias was not solid.

The enemy waited no longer, but began its offensive, counting on all those advantages; one of the pretexts was the Echarate peasant union's execution of a traitorous Aprista bureaucrat in the manor house where he had taken refuge. The stepped-up repression included jailing the leaders, installing posts of Civil Guards in the most militant zones, and so forth. The government defended outrages committed by the *gamonales,* but took bloody reprisals against a peasant meeting in Cuzco.

They didn't touch Chaupimayo, but everyone knew that it would be the target of the last and most ferocious stage of the repression.

We had to choose between dying of malaria and going down fighting. We chose the latter, not through romanticism, but for a political reason. We considered it necessary to educate the masses, to show them how the peasantry must fight the armed force of the enemy even to the last; to show them that although the peasant fell under bullets, the enemy could meet the same fate; to show them that the military uniform is largely a fetish, that it is not an impenetrable armor, as the people tend subconsciously to believe.

All this was so much the more important because the Stalinists were shooting off their mouths that the repression was the result of a premeditated provocation by the Trotskyists, headed by "Hugo Blanco, the well-known international agent of imperialism." We had to defend not only the honor of Trotskyism, but also the honor of the revolution itself from the attack of the opportunists. Against the reformists we had to defend the revolutionary methods to their ultimate consequences.

Besides, there was a real possibility that if the repression against the peasantry and the people in general went to its

ultimate consequences, the guerrilla struggle would be strengthened. The repressive action was limited, however; the peasants were not evicted from land they had won; instead, they
were allowed to remain.

The enemy used the Stalinists cleverly, half as victim and
half as brake: as victim, so as not to discredit them completely, so that they could serve as a brake. It is a reactionary
maneuver, well-known all over the world, that has been carried out not only by utilizing the Stalinists but also other opportunist currents or isolated bureaucrats.

Frankly, our analysis of the situation was not very clear
at the time. In the dynamic of the struggle, the necessity of
imbuing the peasants with optimism fills one with a greater
optimism than would result from an absolutely unemotional
analysis. Not having a party organization, as was the case
in La Convención, aggravated this phenomenon.

Nevertheless, I still think that it was correct to choose the
armed confrontation, even if all the guerrillas had been massacred and the repression against the peasants had been even
more severe. The error was not in turning to guerrilla warfare. It was in having neglected from the start to build the
party, which would have organized, extended, and centralized all aspects of the struggle (armed struggle among them)
in all their variations.

The immediate motive for the step from militia to guerrilla
band lay in the brutal atrocity committed by a landowner,
accompanied by Civil Guards, at the home of Tiburcio Bolaños, secretary-general of the union of the Qayara hacienda:
they ransacked his house, stealing money and furnishings
and abusing his family. The landlord, in the presence of the
Guards, put the barrel of one of their guns to the chest of a
child, threatening to shoot if the child didn't tell where Bolaños could be found, although the child didn't know his where-
abouts. The landlord then propped the gun barrel on the child's
arm and fired.

This news arrived almost simultaneously with news of the
heightened repression in the rest of La Convención and Lares
and of the massacre at the Cuzco meeting at which Remigio
Huamán was killed. We convoked an assembly of the Chaupimayo union, broadened to include comrades from other unions.
Before this assembly, the secretary-general of Qayara stated
his case. We added to this the news of the other events in the
escalated repression and the necessity of confronting it.

The peasants grasped the extreme importance of the case.
Therefore, when they agreed to send a commission to Qayara,

they authorized it not only to bear arms, as was the custom in those cases, but expressly "to make use of them if necessary." Also, contrary to usual practice, they named me, a fugitive, to head the commission. In a still further departure from tradition, they authorized me to decide the size and composition of the commission, as well as the date and hour of departure. Although for a while the peasants had been accustomed to call the militiamen "guerrillas," in reality the guerrilla band was born at that moment, although they called it a commission.

I gathered together the commission, which decided to adopt the name of Remigio Huamán Brigade, in deference to the formal resolution of the federation on Union Defense Brigades and in homage to the peasant murdered at the Cuzco meeting. We departed, armed and carrying guerrilla equipment on our backs.

We never reached Qayara. Faced with the stupidity of the police at the Pujiura post, who believed that "the Indian never shoots," we were forced into our first armed clash, with the result that a policeman was shot. (He turned out to be one of those who had committed the Qayara atrocity.) After finding a doctor in the town and leaving the wounded policeman in his hands, we took refuge in the mountains, taking along the weapons from the police post. (In Pujiura we had learned that the *gamonal* Paullo was no longer at his hacienda, having fled to Cuzco.)

We passed through the valley of San Miguel, where there were the small haciendas where the union movement had not yet penetrated. One of them, populated with peasants from a large hacienda, called a meeting and sent out a delegation to find us. An assembly of peasants from the hacienda was then conducted with our help. Indeed — in addition to the fact that we carried weapons — never had a peasant union in that zone been organized with the help of such a union commission: it included the organizational secretary of the provincial federation, the secretary of agrarian reform of the departmental federation, the secretary of agrarian reform with ties to four unions, two secretaries-general, and other leaders as well.

The newly organized union agreed to apply the agrarian reform decree that we were spreading and which had been put into effect in other zones. They agreed in addition to take into their jurisdiction all the peasants of that valley, since the other haciendas there were somewhat too small to have their own unions.

Another agreement was to go in unison to communicate these new developments to the landlord. We recommended that no measures be taken against him, since he had not been an exceptionally cruel man, and until then had limited himself to profiting from the unequal relations of production.

Although it had been our practice to confiscate the wealth of the big *gamonales* long before we became militiamen, on this occasion we did not touch a thing belonging to the small landowners of the zone. This was not from fear of the repression, for we knew now that the authorities were out to kill us; rather, it was because we were unionists, accustomed to respect the will of the masses, and, as revolutionaries, our military function was nothing more than a small aspect of our political function. And our political function was to teach the workers that *they* had to govern and that we were no more than their military arm, their instrument of struggle, not their benevolent despots.

The peasants had agreed to provide us with everything we would need and to accept anything the small local landowners might voluntarily offer us, but not to confiscate anything from them. As they said, "so that they will see that what we want is the land to work, but that we are not thieves who will steal their belongings." We fulfilled our duty by informing them about our broad policy of confiscating the wealth of the more notoriously villainous landlords, showing them that our agrarian reform decree, despite its combined character, allowed the choice of complete confiscation and that the decree underscored the power of the peasants of the respective haciendas to decide in each specific case the question of measures of confiscation and the manner of distributing the land. It was understood that the existence of the guerrilla bands was not to substitute for the will of the peasants, but to defend and uphold it.

The comrades of San Miguel understood perfectly.

Of course, the landlords had no other recourse than to declare that they would respect the will of the Assembly.

Subsequently, we called a meeting with the small landowners of the zone to explain to them that although the initial revolutionary measures affected them directly, the revolution was not against them; proof of this was that the peasants of the zone had ordered us not to touch them. On the contrary, we were aware that the bourgeois state extracted taxes from them and imposed unjust regulations on production without giving any assistance to the valley; that, faced with this, the peasants had decided to provide from their own resources the area's most urgent needs: roads, a school, a medical clinic; that it was their obligation to work with the peasants in that effort; that, in return, they would not have to pay any debts to the bourgeois banks, nor taxes to the bourgeois state.

We knew that their agreement with our words was no more

sincere than the help they offered us. The concrete and immediate thing for them, although they did not say so, was that we had "taken away their land to give it to the Indians." But it was our political duty to explain to them the broad character of the revolution that would benefit them enormously.*

Then we went to the unionized zones and were joined by a secretary-general, and then by other union leaders. The support of the peasants was almost absolute, and touching. They fed us, clothed us, guided and protected us.

"Eat and take as much as you can," the women would tell us, weeping. "Ay! We are so comfortable in our houses, and you are being hunted on the mountains. How sad it is not to be able to serve you each day like this when you are on the mountain! Comrades! Brothers!" As our stomachs and knapsacks were of limited capacity, we accepted a little from each one, lest anyone should feel offended.

Any suggestion of payment would have been an insult. How could we pay them if we were their military arm? Can a brother who fights for his brother pay him for the food he eats while fighting? Wouldn't that mean we were fighting for someone else? It would have been a grave political error to suggest paying. Only once did we feel obliged to persuade a comrade that he had to accept money from us. That was a peasant who lived in an isolated hut in the *puna,* the frigid zone. He gave us a small bull. We explained to him that for cases like this the comrades had furnished us with money, because it would be wrong for so great an expense to fall upon a single peasant.

We guerrillas were not the ones to explain to the peasants that we fought for them; they themselves told it to us; the immediate reason for our struggle was as clear as water — our unionizing efforts over the past few years explained it abun-

---

* The Stalinists, of the Moscow as well as the Peking variety, view this social sector as a part of the revolutionary forces that must not be adversely affected in the least in this first stage.

This is absurd. If one is on the side of the peasants, one necessarily comes into conflict with this sector, and precisely at the beginning of the process. Their conservative and reactionary position is not determined solely by their economic level, which can be lower than that of the tenant farmer or the small landowner who works his land himself. Their position is determined by the role they play in the productive process, by their opposition to the immediate demands of their tenants, although these may number only two or three. Even before demanding that the land belong to whoever tills it, the peasant comes into conflict with the landlord, no matter how small the latter may be, when he asks for a rent reduction or for the

dantly, and the composition of the band substantiated it. For this reason, our political work touched on even higher subjects: an explanation of the general significance of the revolution and the economic and political tasks we had to accomplish.

I will not recount the days of hunger and thirst during which we rationed our maize, counting the grains, ate wild herbs and quenched our thirst with the liquid found only in certain leaves, the juice of some thistles, or of orchid bulbs. These and other vicissitudes are common to any guerrilla experience.

Because of the lack of a party organization in the zone, all aspects of peasant aid were direct or were channeled through the unions. This was an enormous disadvantage, considering that however well established a mass organization may be, it cannot approach the discipline and discretion of a party organization — vital qualities in such situations.

Even in the guerrilla band, I continued, in my capacity of secretary of agrarian reform of the departmental federation, to sign specific decrees that had been approved by the peasants.

The guerrilla band had two further armed confrontations. In one of them, two enemies fell; and in the other, they put us to flight.

There were isolated actions of peasant sabotage in our behalf (cutting telegraph wires, destroying bridges, for instance). But the great opportunities for sabotage, for the formation of militias and other guerrilla bands, based on the high level of

---

eight-hour work day. In this conflict, the Trotskyists have declared that we are on the side of the poor peasant.

The case of those tenants who — although they exploit other tenants — are themselves directly exploited by the *gamonal* is different and is explained in a preceding chapter. Our correct policy toward them, without capitulation, determined the success of the united front in La Convencion and Lares. A number of such farmers were members of the guerrilla band.

The different positions of the Trotskyists and the Stalinists with regard to the peasants is not an isolated matter, but originates in the different positions of Trotsky and Stalin. The Stalinists accused Trotsky of "turning his back on the peasantry," of using the term *kulak* or rich peasant, whose interests were opposed to those of the poor peasants, as a synonym for *peasant.* It was precisely the *kulaks* who were one of the bulwarks for the attack on Trotsky, although Stalin was later forced to deal with them in a bloody confrontation.

This myth that Trotskyists "underestimate the peasantry" is still repeated to the present day. When we went to the city with some peasant comrades, we had the pleasure of hearing it from the Stalinist university students [H. B.].

the peasants, were tragically lost because of the absence of a
party organization. A favorable atmosphere existed throughout
the country, but there was no organization to make the most of
it for the benefit of the peasant fighters.

Another favorable factor that must be singled out is the
Cuban assistance: it seems that the comrades made tremendous
efforts to have human and material aid sent to us, but nothing
arrived. Even if it had arrived, it would not have saved the
guerrilla band, for the fundamental weakness was political:
a party cannot be imported.

The tremendous Cuban aid that *was* sent to us was the over-
seas voice of Radio Havana. It was enthusiastic and fervent
assistance, that filled us with emotion and reinforced our reso-
luteness. That is why we become so disheartened now when we
hear Radio Havana supporting the military government instead of supporting the daily revolutionary work against the
military government, which represents the exploiters.

In conclusion, we reiterate: the lack of a party was the chief
cause of the destruction of the movement, including the guerrilla bands, as much because it would have immediately filled
our lack with the best kind of support apparatus, as because
its absence as an instrument was the main cause of the isolation of our peasant movement.

We have learned the lesson.

Putschism

The Cuban Revolution opened a new chapter in Latin America. It was a tremendous blow not only to imperialism and
all exploiting classes, but also to reformism of all varieties.
It proved that the Latin American revolution is a socialist
revolution, that this revolution will not be made by peaceful
means, and that it is indeed necessary to destroy — not reform —
the capitalist system.

In this respect, it signified a reaffirmation of Marxist principles, which the Trotskyists had defended during the bleakest
periods of the world revolution. In this respect also, it signified a milestone with regard to the tactic of guerrilla warfare, especially valuable for the colonial and semicolonial
countries.

Other positive milestones can certainly be enumerated with
respect to the first socialist revolution in our hemisphere. Nevertheless, along with its invaluable positive influence on America
and the world, it had some negative effects in the radical movement. Of course, the Cuban Revolution is not to blame for

this, but rather that we revolutionaries lacked dialectical maturity and were not equal to the interpretation of such a sweeping and contradictory process.

The Latin American Trotskyist movement, enthusiastic as it was about this revolution which confirmed the theory of the permanent revolution,[2] could not remain immune from the negative influences, and was also affected by them in various degrees. We can enumerate the most important characteristics of this negative influence: the underestimation of the Leninist principle of constructing a Bolshevik-type party as a fundamental instrument for making the revolution; the underestimation of the transitional program, substituting for it the so-called strategy of armed struggle, or even the strategy of guerrilla warfare; the substitution of audacious actions by a courageous group for mass actions.

I think, although some comrades do not agree with this estimation, that even the leadership of the Latin American Secretariat of Orthodox Trotskyism (SLATO) felt this influence, although it was mitigated by the theoretical level of this leadership.

This tendency was stronger in Comrade Pereyra, who was sent to reinforce our work. For this reason, along with the positive accomplishments of his work, there was the negative influence of his putschist pressure, which is the name given to this deviation because of its characteristic reliance on the blows struck by individual hands.[3]

When I speak of a putschist deviation, I am not referring of course to our armed struggle and its preparation, to the militias and the guerrilla bands. All this comes well within our conception. I believe that our activity in this area was, in general, correct.

Some activities that can be pointed to as examples of putschist pressure are: the bank holdups; the lack of emphasis on building the party; certain attempts to hasten artificially the process of party-building in some instances in the months before the fall of Pereyra; a lack of extended analysis of each phase. Fortunately, we did not succumb to the pressures for an assault on general military headquarters in Cuzco, nor to other extreme expressions of this current.

The credit for reacting first and beginning a serious struggle against this deviation goes to Comrade Nahuel Moreno, the principal theorist of Latin American Trotskyism.

7

Our Trial

The judicial oppression of the Peruvian peasantry is constant, sometimes accompanied by armed repression. After each massacre of peasants, the government brings charges of an attack by armed force against those peasants, including the wounded, who escaped death. In some cases, the police seek out a person who has assumed care of the orphans of the victims, and vent their fury on him or her. (Santiago Arroyo of Ongoy was arrested for having taken charge of raising his brother's children after his brother had been murdered by the police.)

Throughout the whole peasant mobilization process in the department of Cuzco, the judicial authorities were especially active, blaming a multitude of crimes on union leaders. When the armed repression was intensified, the judicial repression increased proportionately, filling the jails with union activists.

Among all these cases, full of judicial abuses, the one that aroused the most interest was the proceedings against members of our guerrilla band, including peasants who had had nothing to do with our activities.

The legal abuses were clear from the start. We were tried by a military tribunal. The judge was an official who specialized in directing massacres, and the members of the tribunal were also the intellectual inspirers of many such massacres.

The tortures to which the prisoners were subjected took place not only when they were interrogated by the police, but even during the arraignments of the accused before the judge. Such was the case with Fortunato Torres, tortured during his arraignment by order of the judge, Mayor Apaésteguia. This was in the presence of the judge, the secretary, who was recording the legal proceedings but not the torture, and another official who was acting as "defense" lawyer for Fortunato Torres.

In the peasants' arraignments, the military judge had anything he pleased entered as their statements; the majority of them could not understand a word of Spanish. During the proceedings, the confrontations required by law did not take place (*careo,* or confrontation of accused by witnesses). Nor were the alleged crimes listed, despite the gravity of the case.

I was held almost completely incommunicado until the day of my audience (oral proceedings). They took special care to keep me apart from my comrades, and they applied continual pressure to persuade them to declare that they had been led astray and to blame me for everything that my accusers wanted them to; thus, they were told, they could save their own skins.

Dr. Victor Angles, my lawyer in Cuzco, and Dr. Alfredo Battilana, my lawyer in Lima, were jailed. They sent Dr. Angles to a prison in the *selva,* and when they let him out, they forbade him to leave the department of Cuzco.

The law required that the audience had to take place by the end of six months after the beginning of the proceedings; nevertheless, it took place only after three years had passed. The causes of the delay were the government's attempts to "persuade" the defendants and witnesses and its hope that public excitement over the case would cool down.

According to the law, the audience would have to take place in Cuzco, capital of the department where the alleged crimes took place, or in Arequipa, seat of the tribunal. Nevertheless, the enemy decided not to conduct it in either of these cities, but in Tacna, where the left was practically nonexistent.

My lawyer discovered the date and place of the audience in an extra-official way. The authorities were trying to impede the defense efforts of Dr. Battilana as well as those of my comrades' lawyers (Dr. Laura Caller and Dr. Marcial Chalco) in order to force us to accept court-appointed lawyers. Only the tenacity and courage of our lawyers was able to surmount this obstacle and make the government respect their rights and ours.

The tribunal did not permit the appearance of any witnesses, not even those who were against us, such as the police who had participated in the encounter at Pujiura, or the doctor to whom we had brought the wounded policeman. The reason was clear: their statements had been prepared by superior officers, and they were sure that the witnesses could not make the "statements" in front of us. Nor were the medical authorities called who had performed the autopsies and presented the "report," which had also been prepared by the superior officers, in which they had described ax murders and other barbarities which are characteristic of the repressive forces in charge of martyring and destroying men, but not of the revolutionaries who fired only to prevent enemy bullets from wounding us, and who treated a wounded enemy as a brother.

In the cell in Tacna, I was kept apart from my comrades and watched by the Republican Guard. The audience, which lasted several days, took place in the headquarters of the Civil Guard squadron.

The Civil Guards, as well as the Republican Guard, displayed great hostility to us at first, regarding us as assassins of their comrades. Even most of the people of Tacna, influenced by the massive propaganda campaign of the bourgeois press and radio, viewed us at first with hostility or indifference.

The first indication that things would not go as the military authorities had planned occurred when my comrades, entering the courtroom, crowded around me spontaneously and embraced me; the guards were unable to prevent this. It was a good demonstration of how futile the officials' three years of work in persuasion had been.

When the president of the military tribunal declared the audience convened, I stood up and in a loud voice challenged his qualifications for judging us. I declared that the servants of the *gamonales* could not constitute themselves as accusers and judges of the peasants; that the bloody-handed assassins of the peasants could not constitute themselves as judges of their victims; that anyone who would sell his country for a few pieces of gold could not judge those of us who fought for national sovereignty.

At the conclusion of that first session, I shouted our slogan: "Land or Death!" And just as in public demonstrations and in the guerrilla band, the comrades responded in chorus: "*Venceremos!*" [We will win!] That showed them how the audience was going to be conducted.

In the following days, the few statements that we had made while accompanied by our lawyers were read aloud and oral statements were made by the comrades. In each case, the profound social roots of the events were made clear. Each peasant denounced the atrocities of which he, his family, and other peasants had been victims. They testified that they had helped demand justice and that the authorities had made the victims of the *gamonales,* not the *gamonales* themselves, bear the brunt of their power. They showed that they had had to resort to organizing themselves in unions, defending their constitutional rights, and that those unions were not recognized but were suppressed and the leaders jailed. They denounced the fierce wave of repression that had been instituted against the peasants of the region and said that they had no alternative but to take up arms and face death, as the only possible way of defending their rights.

And when they were asked about me, they praised me to the skies, attributing to me merits that I certainly don't possess. None of them pleaded that they had been tricked by the agitators, as the enemy had sought to get them to say (with the promise that they would acquit anyone who said so). Even the peasants who had been arbitrarily included in the case, and who had not participated in the guerrilla band, became accusers of *gamonalismo* and the repression.

As the days passed, a change in the attitude of the Tacna population toward us became noticeable: indifference and suspicion shifted to support, to touching and passionate massive solidarity. The courtroom would be filled, and many people who could not get in waited expectantly in the street. When we were taken from the courtroom to the cells, or back, we were accompanied by ovations from the people. They brought food, clothing, and other presents to the cells. The hotel workers paid for our lawyers' room and board.

An old man stopped Dr. Battilana on the street and told him with tears in his eyes, "Tell Blanco that if he has to die, then let him die, but he must not sell out!" It was the voice of my people, victims of the infirmity of APRA, in which they had put their confidence, victims of the treason of the Communist Party and of how many others. A people fighting for centuries and still without the consistent vanguard organization that their courage deserves.

Even the Civil Guards and Republican Guards changed their attitudes radically. They realized that what we were saying was not directed against them, but against their superiors. "Give them hell, brother!" they would tell me.

When it was my turn to make a statement, the tribunal would not permit me to refer to the outrages by the landlords and the authorities, saying that they had already heard that from my codefendants and that I must "stick to the concrete facts."

Within the "facts," I explained that in all senses and at all times, we had acted only in self-defense; that not only had the origin and activity of the guerrilla band been defensive acts in the face of the repression, but also that in our encounters with the police we had saved our lives by firing. This was indisputable. Nor could anyone deny that we never intended to kill anyone, as we proved by our treatment of the policeman who had fired at us in Pujiura — after we had disarmed him, we set him free. Nor could our concern in helping

Blanco protesting the injustice of the trial

Blanco with his defense lawyer, Alfredo Battilana

Peasant militants from the Remigio Huamán Defense Brigade on trial in Tacna. Blanco appears at the extreme left of the second row of defendants.

the wounded be denied, as was shown by the fact that we forced the town doctor (after getting him out from under his bed, where he had been hiding) to treat the wounded police-man, and that we offered our own scanty medical supplies for first aid; all this was done at grave risk to our safety and lives.

Of course, the tribunal was deaf, but the population of Tacna was not.

Besides all this, still within the bounds of "the concrete facts," there were two "doctrinal" points that were unavoidable: The tribunal asked me what I said to Tiburcio Bolaños when he told me about the atrocities perpetrated against his family. Just as I had given Tiburcio Bolaños an explanation of the class character of bourgeois justice and the unavoidable ne-cessity for the people to arm themselves to get justice, I repeated the explanation in great detail before the attentive public.

Another question concerned my words to the policeman we had captured. Again, in full detail, I repeated the explanation that I had given him: that the ranks of the army and police are part of the exploited population, used by the exploiters to maintain social injustice; that, as any guardsman could tell, the officers, besides being abusive and very powerful, enjoyed all the privileges and all the honors, while the troops, in miserable conditions, took all the risks; that it was nec-essary and incumbent upon the troops to join the struggle of their brother workers against the handful of exploiters. This especially disturbed the tribunal, because both Civil Guards and Republican Guards were on duty in the room. Neverthe-less, they had to let me speak, for I was "dealing strictly with concrete facts."

At the end of my explanation, the president of the tribunal asked me if I had anything further to add. I declared that if my work to promote social justice deserved the death sen-tence, which Fernando Hernani, one of the members of the tribunal, had demanded, then I was prepared to receive it; but that I demanded that Fernando Hernani carry it out with his own hands, so that my blood would not stain the hands of any Civil or Republican Guard, for they were sons of the people.

Since I had said this in a loud voice, and gestured toward the guards present, the president shouted orders to take me from the room. The strong defense put up by our lawyers was received with warm applause by the public, which caused the president to threaten to clear the courtroom.

In the face of the international, national, and local pressure, they did not sentence me to death but to twenty-five years' imprisonment. When the sentence was read and they asked me if I was in agreement with the verdict, I declared that I would testify to the irregularity of a tribunal that was both an interested party and a judge; that we, the revolutionaries, would have to answer for our deeds before our people, and that the people of Tacna had already given their verdict.

Several comrades gave cheers for the revolution and shouts of "Land or Death!" that were answered by the people with "Venceremos!" Amid the applause and the ovations of the public, the president again cleared the courtroom.

In hopes that the populace would get discouraged and go away, they did not take us back to our cells until the middle of the night. Nevertheless, the people waited until that late hour to give us their vocal encouragement. On the only day that they permitted us to receive visitors, there were hundreds of people who wanted to show their support, but only a small part of them could get in to see us.

The newspaper *Tacera* devoted an issue to the proceedings, bringing us the ardent support of Tacna. Even the bourgeois dailies and radio stations had to modify their attitude toward us, noting tacitly or explicitly that we had not taken up arms because we like the smell of gunpowder, but because of the barbarous conditions of social injustice upheld by the authorities.

After being transferred from the jail at Tacna to this island [El Frontón Prison Island], I was again threatened with the death sentence. The public prosecutor of the Supreme Court of Military Justice asked for it.

Because of this new threat, the worldwide campaign against the death sentence was intensified. That campaign, initiated by the Trotskyist comrades, and carried on by revolutionaries of all tendencies and by all those who considered the sentence unjust, was responsible for saving my life. (This is not to say that Dr. Battilana's defense was not brilliant.) That campaign was an indication of the power of international solidarity.

That campaign showed that it is possible to stay the assassins' hands and that it is our obligation to extend the struggle on a global scale to stop Yankee genocide in Indochina.

Many people do not understand why the present government, which is interested in liquidating the old agrarian structure, imprisoned us for participating in the peasant struggle for that liquidation, and why the *gamonal* Luna Oblitas and many other mass murderers of peasants enjoy their liberty.

Government spokesmen make a distinction, a mechanical separation, between my "socially useful work" and the "murder" represented by the death of the police. This explanation becomes more incomprehensible in the mouths of those who are now trying to invoke the memory of Túpac Amaru[1] who committed many murders beginning with that of Magistrate Arriaga, a representative of authority and the established order. They recognize that "formerly the armed forces were utilized to defend the interests of the oligarchy," that "the revolution cannot be based on the institutions of the past." They declare that "if anyone opposes the revolution, blood will flow," and that "if the oligarchy succeeds in dividing the armed forces, there will be civil war."

Within this conception, as can be seen, the separation between socially useful work and murder becomes ridiculous, if the spilling of blood occurs during the process of socially useful work and as a regrettable but inescapable consequence thereof.

The mystery is unveiled when it is described clearly: the government is interested in liquidating the old agarian structure in order to make capitalism more dynamic, to give modern form to the exploitation of the Peruvian workers. Yet the capitalist and his government are fundamentally tied to the *gamonal* who murders peasants. In the final instance, they are also his government, since they are looking for the best way to maintain the exploitation of man by man.

On the other hand, despite their superficial similarities with the revolutionary socialists regarding the agrarian problem, the *gamonales* look upon us as their true enemies, as extremists who fight to the end to liquidate the exploitation of man by man, and not simply to modernize or reform that exploitation, as they do. This explains why we revolutionaries are the ones imprisoned for fighting against the oligarchy, and not Luna Oblitas, Alfredo Romainville, and the other assassins of the workers of the countryside.

8

Some Questions Answered

This chapter endeavors to give answers to a comrade who read the manuscript and had some questions. [H. B.]

Repression Against the FIR

The FIR had not penetrated the mass movement sufficiently and for that reason it was unable to withstand the repression of May 1962, and was easily destroyed. Only the small part of the party that was in the countryside was able to withstand it (and even that was smashed a few months later in the bloody repression against the entire peasant movement of which it was the vanguard).

It is understood that I am speaking of a temporary defeat. The FIR, which has its roots in the countryside and which penetrates more and more deeply into the struggle of exploited Peru, can no longer be liquidated.

Strengthening of Opportunism

With the retreat of the masses, the opportunists became stronger, not only because the militant vanguard was swept away, but because opportunism thrives most on the fearfulness of the masses and on the mood of defeat which predominates in such periods. In periods of upsurge, the revolutionary currents become stronger because they harmonize with the combative spirit of the masses, acting as its cause and effect.

The Influence of Our Movement Outside the Zone

The consciousness of the peasantry in the adjacent regions and in other zones rose notably. The influence of La Convención and Cuzco was noted in the massive land seizures ("invasions") in subsequent years in various zones of the country. Unfortunately, these magnificent spontaneous mobilizations suffered grievously from the same shortcomings as those in

La Convención and Cuzco: the lack of a revolutionary party.

La Convención and Cuzco also influenced the heightening of the revolutionary consciousness of the students and the urban population in general. After decades of opportunist reformism, the people saw a leftist movement that demonstrated a will to insurrection. This dealt a formidable blow to the anti-Trotskyist sectarianism which had formerly predominated in a leftist movment that had imbibed all of its Marxism at the founts of Stalinism. It made known the wretched conditions existing in the countryside to urban Peru and to the world.

The bourgeois governments were forced to take a series of reform measures of benefit to the peasants in order to alleviate the tension. The principal measures are the agrarian reform laws: the *Ley de Bases* of the preceding junta, Belaúnde's law, and finally the law of the present junta (the other causes of these laws are the needs of the pro-development bourgeoisie). They also made many improvements in public health, roads, education, and so forth; although what they increased most, of course, were police stations. It is interesting to note that for many years my union had demanded that they enforce the law that obliged Romainville to support a school; then, when we set one up ourselves, we demanded that he finance it. None of this was done; subsequently, when Chaupimayo was no longer demanding that he finance the school, the state did it.

My Specific Function as Under-Secretary and Later Secretary of Press and Propaganda

Much can be accomplished in press and propaganda work even in such a predominantly illiterate milieu as the peasant movement.

It is necessary to understand that for centuries the oppressors of the peasants made them regard paper as a god. Paper became a fetish: Arrest orders are paper. By means of papers they crush the Indian in the courts. The peasant sees papers in the offices of the governor, the parish priest, the judge, the notary — wherever there is power; the landowner, too, keeps accounts on paper. All the reckonings you have made, all your logical arguments, they refute by showing you a paper; the paper supersedes logic, it defeats it.

There is a famous saying: *Qelqan riman* [What is written is what is heard]. We fight this fetishism to the death. And one of the ways to fight it is precisely to show the peasant that, just as the enemy has *his* papers, so we have *our* papers.

To the paper that contradicts the reason and logic of the peasant, we counterpose the paper that bears that reason and logic.

This by itself is already a marvel for the illiterate peasant. The existence of papers that speak in his behalf, that speak his truth, is already the beginning of his triumph. He views them with respect and affection.

The peasants have always pasted papers on the walls of their homes. This time they did it in a special way. It was touching to come across those yellowing leaflets on the stick and straw walls of the huts of the *puna*. Besides, some children and some visitors, too, can read them, filling the inhabitant of the hut with pride at each reading.

Another important function of the position of press and propaganda secretary was to expose the harsh reality of the peasants' lives to the urban population. When Chaupimayo bought an old mimeograph machine, it was a great leap forward. The peasants from the various unions saw with happiness that simply by using the proper amount of paper and ink, they could make their problems known to everyone, could have their own leaflet, could print a paper listing the name of the landowner, his crimes, his accomplices, and his victims. This gave them new strength, new determination.

The landowners were so spineless that even though the administration of justice was in their hands, and they could easily have jailed me on a slander charge for signing these exposés, they never did. Each landowner knew that although it could cost me a jail sentence, it would cost him our special attention in demonstrating before public opinion that all these exposés were true and that there were many others as well. None of them wanted to become more famous than the others through this publicity, which did not respect the oldest and most illustrious names, until then untouched and venerated.

Unfortunately, we did not get to utilize posters, which, as the Russian Revolution showed, are especially useful in areas with a high percentage of illiteracy.

Participation of Non-Peasant Elements in the Agrarian Movement of That Period

In addition to the members of the directorate of the FTC and its lawyers, most of these elements belonged to the opportunist current; when the movement grew, there was collaboration from the comrades of the FIR and some other elements of radical youth.

Comrades Gorki Tapia and Juvenal Zamalloa worked actively with me in La Convención and Lares; Gorki was named dentist of the federation; Ronald Rosas, Salustio Jiménez, Huarcaya Gamarra and perhaps some others were in the mountain areas of the department; Urbano López (who was not in the FIR) was in Pillpinto and Lares; the lawyer Estenio Pacheco (also not in the FIR) was in La Convención and Lares. Pereyra and Aragón collaborated from the city.

All this was before the repression of the FIR. Subsequently, Comrade Blanca La Berrera from July to November of 1962 worked in the embryonic party organization in Chaupimayo, in the night school, and then in Lares, where soon after she fell prisoner during the repression directed against the vanguard of that valley.

Pedro Candela (a fugitive because of his participation in the bank expropriation) collaborated in the military aspect, with his ex-soldier's know-how in weapons training and in the guerrilla band. Months after the November intensification of the repression against the peasant movement, comrades Vladimiro Valer and Héctor Loayza participated in leading the movement's resurgence in the department. They can tell who worked in that period with Urbano López.

It is possible that some names have been accidentally omitted here.

Organization of the Unions

I was just another of the union organizers of the FPCC and of the FDCC. The organization of peasant unions in the department was begun much earlier under the FTC. There had even been militant peasant unions then. It can be said that the old-time militancy of the peasantry had also expressed itself in union form. Evidence of this was the Peasant Union of San Jerónimo in the 1940s led by Lorenzo Chamorro.

I did not participate in the first — rather weak — work stoppage in La Convención (that day I was arrested for leading a picket line in the city of Cuzco). One of the leaders of the work stoppage was Comrade Fortunato Vargas.

The peasant strike was at Pachachaca Grande, sparked by Comrade Aniceto Muñoz. The armed resistance of the peasantry — aside from the famous uprisings in history — took isolated, sporadic, continuing forms. A good example in La Convención is the execution of the *gamonal* Alberto Duque on the eve of the union movement.

Our participation was not so much to initiate or introduce class-struggle tactics, which were spontaneous in large measure, but to systematize them and make people conscious of them, since Marxism had enabled us to understand the class struggle and to see which of the tactics used by the peasantry would be effective for its liberation. We adopted those tactics, we added to them, we perfected them, we integrated them into a strategy; we practiced and advocated them systematically.

It can be said that we represented the fusion of the militant form of peasant struggle with the Marxist conception and experience, with a consciousness of the significance of this struggle. We were, in a word, the representatives of the party (with all its deficiencies) in this zone, the conscious factor in the workers' struggle.

Assaults on the Banks and Police Headquarters in Cuzco

In principle, we are not against such activities as assaults on banks and police headquarters; they are a part of the revolutionary struggle, of the war of the people against their enemies. But more precisely, they must be the fruit of the growing class consciousness of the people. When the maturity of consciousness of the masses brings them to understand the necessity of these activities, it is correct to engage in them. The secrecy and discretion that are absolutely essential in such cases does not contradict this; for we do not mean to say that the masses must be informed before all actions, but that these actions must be carried out when the masses have arrived at an understanding of their necessity and regard them as their own acts, as *their* forms of struggle.

This applies not only to the question of whether such activites are necessary, for in general all of them are always "necessary," since the revolutionary movement always needs money and arms. It applies fundamentally to the political impact of such acts. If they are done when the people understand their necessity and they are understood by the masses as activities emanating from themselves, they fulfill above all the positive function of raising the consciousness of the masses, increasing their self-confidence, when they see themselves as the author of those deeds.

On the other hand, if they are carried out when the masses have not yet arrived at an understanding of their necessity, they play a negative role, for many reasons, and they are used by the enemy as the ostensible justification for repressive violence. They then endanger courageous revolutionaries. In our case, the very existence of the organization hung in the balance.

Instead of increasing the masses' self-confidence, they cause it to diminish; some are convinced by the reactionary propaganda, and others at least see us as provocateurs, even though they consider our motives justified; finally, and this is very important, even those sectors that have a favorable attitude toward such acts fall back, for they come under the illusion that a group of redeemers will complete the struggle and that consequently the masses do not have to exert themselves to improve their organization or their struggle.

On the subject of redeemers there is more to be said. The bourgeoisie, like the exploiting classes of the past, fosters a belief in redeemers. Basically this belief is similar to religious alienation; it is another opiate of the people. Just as they try to maintain the passivity of the exploited masses with the hope of a Holy Saviour and a future paradise, they also point to leader saviours (Haya, Belaúnde, Odría, Velasco).

It is not necessary that these leaders be right-wingers; the opportunists of the left, who are not controlled by the bourgeoisie, are also used to make the masses believe that such leaders — and not the actions of the masses themselves — are responsible for winning victories for the exploited masses.

The bourgeoisie will even exalt the authentic revolutionaries, even though it may be through insults and slander. They are eager to extol the individual at the expense of the masses. As long as the masses believe in a redeemer, no matter how revolutionary he may be, the bourgeoisie feels relatively secure. This redeemer can be bought off, jailed, or killed; they cannot do this to the masses. On the day that the masses realize that their power lies in themselves, the exploiters are finished. Old Marx was profoundly correct when he said: "The liberation of the workers will be the task of the workers themselves."

Therefore, Marxists persist in showing the masses that their power lies in themselves, in a methodology that sifts the experiences of the world's people, in organizations suitable for actions by the masses. If there are different levels of organization whose vanguard is the party, it is precisely because the party brings together the least alienated and most combative sector of those masses, the sector that believes least in redeemers and that believes most in the power of the masses; the party is not a collection of exceptional individuals who can substitute themselves for the action of the masses.

When in the course of the struggle, the triumphs of our methodology are seen as the individual merit of some comrade, and this view is encouraged by the enemy, our duty is to continue struggling for the disillusionment of the masses, for their disenchantment, to show them that the merit is in the program of struggle and the methods that that comrade has employed and that are based precisely on a profound confidence in the masses. In this way, the most advanced and decisive elements of the masses will understand that they are capable of mastering those methods in their manifold and complete development, but that in order to do so, it is essential to unite and combine their individual forces in a disciplined organization, in the revolutionary party which is characterized by just such methods.

Dr. Battilana's Defense

Dr. Battilana's defense was conducted with simplicity, clarity, and integrity. It was distinguished by being profoundly political. He showed with the strength of logical argument free of pompous rhetoric, that for the peasantry, which sought to achieve a minimum level of human living conditions, all roads were closed, except the one it had taken. His exposition was directed not at the audience's emotions, but at its reason.

While defending me, he had the peasants more at heart than he did me as an individual. At one point he asked me to explain all about the agrarian reform decree I had issued in the name of the peasants (this point had not been previously mentioned). Based on this, he showed that in reality the authorities should have tried me for sedition, as the Legal Code stipulated, because my objective was breaking up established power. He realized that this could damage my case legally, but that it helped to make clear to the people that the logic of the struggle for the satisfaction of their grievances would itself lead them inescapably to the destruction of the bourgeois political system.

My Capture

In January, the repressive forces surprised our guerrilla band, attacking us with a characteristically lavish waste of ammunition; fortunately their aim was so bad that they did not succeed in wounding any of us, although they did succeed in scattering us. After this attack, it proved impossible for me to link up with any of my comrades. Taking the greatest possible precautions, I arrived at the hut of a comrade I did not know. He and his wife had no difficulty in recognizing me and understanding the gravity of the situation. They were able to make some contacts, but without communicat-

ing with any leaders (who were the most closely watched and
frequently attacked). So they took me to a peasant who lived
in a remote place. Near his hut, where from time to time he
left me some food, I survived for a while, alternating his food
with mountain herbs and fasting.

By chance, I ran into a boy, Mario Huamán, who showed
great solidarity. Since no party organization existed in that
zone, it was dangerous to try to enter into contact with the
besieged activists. Mario offered to go to Cuzco, where he
succeeded in getting into contact with the comrades who were
reorganizing the FIR.

Unfortunately, the inexperience of those comrades in work
requiring great secrecy allowed a political infiltrator to get
to know the contact, Mario. It was easy work for the police
to capture and torture the boy to tell where I was. The boy,
who was not a hardened militant and who thought, quite correctly, that if he did not talk, the tortures would continue until
they killed him, provided the information that enabled the
police to capture me. With that information, the police forced
him to act as a guide under threat of death.

They surrounded the place with a great deployment of forces
so that any resistance was impossible, even if I had not been
alone and poorly armed (a rusty revolver, with six dubious
bullets, and a dagger). I hid, but with the number of pur-
suers it was not hard for them to find me. I barely had time
to hide some papers that would have compromised other comrades.

The force was composed of troops of the Civil Guard, who
had orders to shoot to kill me, and members of the Intelligence Police (PIP), with orders to take me alive. The ones
who discovered, bound, and imprisoned me were PIP soldiers; the Civil Guard official who came up to me after I was
already manacled and under guard had to content himself
with hitting me on the head with his rifle butt in the hope
of forestalling any censure for lack of zeal from his superiors
who, like all their type, understand that to kill us legally presents certain difficulties, and so prefer direct assassination.
In this respect, less lucky than Béjar and myself were the comrades De la Puente, Vallejos, Heraud, and many others who
were killed in cold blood after they had been captured, just
as Che was.

So there was no treason by anybody in my capture. There
was negligence, as a result of inexperience, by the Cuzco comrades. We cannot call Mario Huamán a traitor; he was not
a militant, and his only alternative was death. He endured

as much as he could, but they beat him mercilessly. (Fortuately, I managed to send a note explaining this to the cell where other imprisoned comrades were planning reprisals against the boy.)

The FBI openly rewarded the perpetrators of my capture.

But these incidental details about my capture do not go to the root of the matter. The true cause lies in the retreat of the peasant masses who were incapable of confronting the repression because of their isolation and the lack of a party. The scattering of the guerrilla band, my isolation, the inexperience of the comrades, the need to fall back on people who were not in the party, were only symptoms of that grave deficiency.

Part II

Introductory Remarks

It would give me pleasure to reproduce, in the pages that follow, the leaflets, articles, and press communications of the period of the peasant mobilization that this book deals with. Unfortunately, I have none of this material at hand. I have had to resign myself to transcribing some of the articles, letters, and news items dealing with the peasant struggle written on this island in the past few years.

The first were written while the death sentence still hung over my head. I include the "Letter to Those Who Have Protested the Death Sentence" as testimony of my profound gratitude to all those to whom I owe my life. I repeat, making use of this occasion in particular, my heartfelt appreciation of my imprisoned comrades — politically and socially of various tendencies — who, in various prisons, declared a hunger strike to protest the death sentence that threatened me. I include the letter to my peasant comrades, stating that as of that date Comrade Vicente Lanado was still imprisoned.

Most of the writings that figure in the following pages tend, as the reader will see, to encourage the revolutionaries toward working in the arena of the peasant movement.

I have been criticized for giving, in the letter "To My People," an overly optimistic picture and of speaking of the students as though they were already marching with the peasants. I have also been criticized for the "exaggerated modesty" of my letter to the Congress of the Federation of Peruvian Students. I believe that these criticisms are justified. My excuse is that I thought I was actually at death's door; and I was making bold efforts, that might be my last, to pull the revolutionary students into peasant work.

The letter to the FEP was on the occasion of the congress at which the students, in solidarity against the repression, nominated Héctor Béjar and myself. My proposal never reached the discussion stage because of a split in the congress.

Hugo Neyra comments on "the problems of personal communication with the isolated peasantry" of the "young creole, Jorge Carrión, founder of unions," described in the story "Puna." But I have tried to show precisely the possibility that even such an inexperienced and completely urban person as Carrión has of gradually integrating himself with the peasantry. We must keep in mind that besides those completely urban elements, of whom there are many examples, there are also those who are to some extent of peasant origins, as in my case, or who are even pure peasants who came to the cities, and for whom the return presents no particular difficulty.

Without abandoning the perspective, especially for the revolutionary students, of going to the countryside, the FIR members now consider that our principal task as a party is to create a strong urban nucleus with Bolshevik discipline on a fundamentally working-class base; with this base, *centralized* peasant work will be easier and more fruitful. Now that the FIR has cleansed itself, this is possible, proving that it was not that the line was lacking, but rather that many members were somewhat less than true FIRistas.

On rereading Chapter II, I see that I stopped short. I described the productive relations in their bare form without mentioning the complement of those relations, the aspect that does not figure in the contracts (whether written or verbal) — the additional barbaric atrocities committed by the landlords, which are by no means exceptions. I can say that in the story "Puna," I describe the "normal" average. As proof that I do not exaggerate, I submit the leaflet referring to Vicente Lanado and the hacienda Paltaybamba, which, as can be seen, is a truth stranger than the fiction of the story "Puna."

Another example was the hacienda bordering Paltaybamba, Santa Rosa-Chaupimayo, the seat of my union. There the *gamonal* Alfredo Romainville strung up a naked peasant to a mango tree and, among other things, flogged him all day in the presence of his own daughters and other peasants. Another peasant could not find the horse his master had told him to find. Romainville forced him down on all fours, ordered him to put on the horse's harness, and compelled him to haul six *arrobas* [150 pounds] of coffee; he made him travel in this fashion, on hands and knees, around the patio where the coffee was dried, lashing him with a whip. He forced the women to shell peanuts without pay until their hands bled, and then with their mouths until those were bloody too. He had his own daughter, born of a peasant woman he had raped, jailed as a "communist." His brother was not satisfied with raping the peasant women himself — he forced a peasant at gunpoint to rape his own aunt.

The landlord Márquez took the children borne by the women he had raped and drowned them in the river. With a hot cattle-branding iron, the landlord Bartolomé Paz seared onto the buttocks of a peasant the emblem of his hacienda. The landlord Angel Miranda did likewise. The landlord Vitorino printed his own money, so that the peasants would be compelled to buy whatever they needed from his hacienda. Dalmiro Casafranca murdered Erasmo Zuñiga, secretary-general of the union of the hacienda Aranjuez, by throwing him into the river.

These crimes were not punished by the authorities — who were very often the landlords themselves. The judges and the police participated in these crimes and protected the perpetrators. That is the real social context in which we agitators were "disturbing the peace" and "advocating violence."

Open Letter to the
Supreme Court of Military Justice

El Frontón Penal Colony
November 5, 1966

To the President of the Supreme Court of Military Justice

Sir:

Whereas: The signatories below, codefendants of Hugo Blanco Galdós, having recently been informed that State's Attorney Don Ruiz de Samocurcio has asked the death sentence for Hugo Blanco, address ourselves to you for the purpose of requesting that, in the event that the court decrees the said death sentence on our leader, the leader of the entire peasantry of the country, that we too be executed. For we believe that the responsibility for the deeds occasioning this trial cannot be individualized.

Together with Comrade Hugo Blanco, we have fought for national and social liberation not only of the peasantry, but of all exploited classes; and we want to suffer the consequences of this historic struggle together with him.

We interpret the demand of the state's attorney, and the sinister intent that it reflects, as a deplorable vengeance of the *gamonales,* who were beginning to disintegrate in Peru, thus opening a road for the redemption of the Peruvian peasants, who are the basis for the country's economic, social, and cultural development.

If this bunch of privileged idlers wants to spill our blood in a vain attempt to stave off the inevitable insurrection of the workers of city and countryside, and of all conscious Peruvians, let them try. The hour is near when they will have to settle accounts before the Popular Revolutionary Tribunals.

Land or Death! We Will Win!

Gerardo Carpio Molina
José Zuñiga Letona
Lucio Beingolea Torres

Humberto Carazas Moscoso
Aniceto Muñoz Linares
Emiliano Cernades Ojeda

From left to right, Gerardo Carpio, Humberto Carazas, Hugo Blanco, José Zuñiga, and Aniceto Muñoz, imprisoned together at El Frontón Prison Island.

Among the trade-union militants pictured here are Manuel Canal (third from the left) and Andrés Gonzáles (fifth from the right).

Indian peasants at a demonstration

To My People

El Frontón Penal Colony
November 24, 1966

The revolutionary loves life. For, though he suffers intensely his own affliction and the affliction of all his brothers, he lives in order to destroy that affliction. So, despite the suffering, he is happy.

The revolutionary loves the world. For, though he lives in a world of misery, injustice, and hatred; though he feels more keenly than anyone the misery of all humanity, he exists in order to change that world. So, the revolutionary loves the world; for though he lives in an earthly hell, he exists in order to transform it into an earthly paradise. He lives in a world of hatred and strife to turn it into a world of love.

To be a revolutionary is to love the world, to love life, to be happy. So, he doesn't flee from life, he understands that it is his duty to live for the fight, and he enjoys life.

But neither must he flee from death!

Because you can fight as well by dying; you can transform the world as well by dying. Because you can love life as well by dying! Because you live even through death! So, you must also accept death.

And for the Peruvian revolutionary, death is no disgrace. It can be no disgrace that my blood will flow to that red and militant river, wherever the blood of Lucho Zapata, of De la Puente, of Lobatón, of Heraud, of Vallejos, of Velando flows and fights on.

It is no disgrace to give a Land or Death salute to Remigio Huamán in the blood whose origin is the eternal Túpac Amaru.

To die for life, like a Vietnamese fighter, is happiness; to die for the death of imperialism, capitalism, and *gamonalismo;* to die for the death of hunger, misery, and ignorance.

To die is no disgrace when it brings nearer the dawn; when you see, you feel the massive awakening of the peasants; when you see the workers, step by step, reconstructing the true Workers' Union of Mariátegui[1] to sweep away capitalism and all its allies; when you see the students marching hand in hand with workers and peasants, conscious of their historic mission.

A fighting death is no disgrace. For the revolutionary, that is the natural way to die.

How can I not die happy, knowing that before my blood

dries, many "gorillas" [militarists] are preparing to go abroad "for health reasons"—to Miami or some other port for traitors? How can I not die happy, knowing that it will signal the exodus of the *gusanos?*[2] Happy, because my people are showing that the whole Peruvian oligarchy and all its servants will have to pack their bags in a hurry to follow them.

Because the day is near. And they know it too!

Land or Death! We Will Win!

Hugo Blanco Galdós

To the Congress of the Peruvian Federation of Students

Comrade Students:

Now that I am face to face with death, I have been reviewing my life as a peasant, as a worker, and as a student; and it is as a student that I speak to you, comrades; it is from my seat in the lecture hall that I send word to your congress, although I know that I could also do it as a peasant or as a worker.

This is a letter, a message, from a fighter who may have only a few days left, to fighters who are just beginning. This is perhaps something of a confession in this hour of confessions. And to whom can I confess but to my people? And who must absolve me or censure me but my people? And you are my people in embryo.

I conduct this inquiry, perhaps this autopsy, and I give to you the synthesis of my experience; I hope it will be useful. My way of explaining the problem may seem egocentric. But I refer to my personal experience precisely to demonstrate that it was nothing extraordinary, that any of you can accomplish even more with the same effort.

I was a student with below-average abilities, with a below-average cultural level, with many limitations that I still have. My wish was the same as yours: to complete my professional studies in order to serve my people to the best of my abilities.

Then I saw what you are seeing: that becoming a professional meant becoming part of the fabric of a system at the service of the oppressors; that my knowledge would be only to the tiniest degree useful to my people, and to a great degree useful to the enemy's apparatus. I understood that although my country needed technicians, it needed fighters more, fighters who would struggle for a society in which technicians, free of their shackles, could truly serve the people. To fight most efficiently for this transformation I entered the working class; then the peasantry, because I saw that in our country, with its peculiar characteristics, the peasantry, that exploited and hungry class, would be the force that would begin the decisive struggle.

It is up to you to say whether this work was useful to our people. If you believe that it has been, it is your duty to follow it up; I am sure that you will do so a thousand times more effectively and a thousand times more extensively. I know this better than anyone, because I know all my own limitations better than anyone else. I understand better than anyone else that the magnitude achieved in my work was absolutely not a result of any special qualities of my personality, but of the historic moment in which the country is living, in which the fusion of the students with the peasant movement will produce decisive results for the country's future.

The least of your skills is a treasure that will benefit the broad masses of peasants. With what attention and care they will listen! And with what satisfaction will you see your advice take on material form all over the countryside.

And you will see that the peasantry also has a great deal to teach you, quite a bit! And you will respect them more each day.

I can see you already, comrades, walking with the peasants, side by side, perseveringly, learning and teaching, leaving the lowlands to climb the summits with weapons in hand to evict the usurpers.

With regard to this work, which I consider of fundamental importance for the students in this period, I submit a motion. In it I call for twenty comrades — it might just as easily be fifteen or thirty. I specify twenty for a double reason: first, that something very concrete be resolved, that the motion passed not be an abstraction; and second, that it be understood that a very small number of students will have a big effect on the peasant movement.

Motion to the Congress of the FEP

Whereas:

1. The assassination of Comrade Hugo Blanco being prepared by the reaction has as its principal objective to intimidate the Peruvian people, who are fighting for their rights;

Boy playing a *quena* on the road to Cuzco

Lima Committee for Defense of Human Rights sponsored this demonstration in December of 1966 to demand a general amnesty for political prisoners, abolition of the death penalty, an end to repression, and no more "disappearances." Among those political prisoners mentioned on the poster are Blanco, Javier Heraud, and Vicente Lanado.

2. The Peruvian youth must demonstrate through action that the repressive terrorism will not intimidate but rather will stimulate their struggle;

3. The position of the above-named comrade has been, in essence, for students to join the peasant movement;

4. Any student can promote that work with much more effective results for the revolutionary transformation that the country needs;

Therefore be it resolved:

1. To choose a minimum of twenty comrades to join the peasant movement in various zones of the country; participating in it with perseverance from its organizational stage, and more modest and elementary legal conquests, to the seizure of the land and state power, with weapons in hand. These comrades will have to be prepared to leave everything, including their studies, if that is necessary to carry out their work.

2. To make maximum use of vacations to develop this work in a massive way.

3. To provide all the necessary help to the peasant movement, as much in its struggle against the *gamonales* and their servants as in all other aspects of their collective struggle.

Hugo Blanco Galdós
1966

Letter to Those Who Protested the Death Sentence

To the organizations and individuals all over the world who — whether or not they identify with my struggle for socialist revolution — have protested the death sentence being prepared against me by those who oppress my people, the national exploiters and the imperialists:

Your voice of solidarity resounds throughout the world, and the conspiracy of silence imposed by the enemies of humanity has not been able to silence it.

People of all languages, your protest has risen in a chorus of the universal language of human solidarity. A tremendous shout, thundering against death, for real and complete human liberty.

At the root of your decisive rejection of this legal assassination is solidarity with my people who are starving to death, and who are fighting to liberate themselves, solidarity with all colonial and semicolonial countries who are breaking their age-old chains, and with mankind in general, fighting to achieve abundance in a complete and universal brotherhood.

We are not strangers, we are brothers. We are strongly united by confidence in humanity and its future; by optimism regarding the positive results of the transformation that will liquidate all inhumanity.

Even if the enemy does succeed in this assassination, you will have triumphed, for your activity shows the road to be followed, and human solidarity will be greatly strengthened.

With your example, solidarity will extend to all the political prisoners of Peru; to the victims of repression in Latin America and in all the countries fighting to liberate themselves; to the people who fight to maintain their independence, as in Cuba. Solidarity with the Vietnamese people, to whom the human race owes so much, will increase beyond measure.

If my murder is carried out, I will die certain that your powerful voice will stop many assassins' bullets and will tear down their jails.

If these criminals don't kill me, it will not be because they lack the desire, but because of the power of your solidarity.

With a heartfelt and fraternal embrace,

Hugo Blanco Galdós
1967

Puno

El Frontón Penal Colony
June 1967

"All the town officials, *aliancistas,* [1] coalition supporters, and independents agreed to the strike"; "peasants at Ayaviri tore up the railroad tracks"; "all the means of communication are cut."

These and similar news bulletins informed us of the work stoppage in the department of Puno. [2] It was a total strike that closed shops, warehouses, markets. A total strike that permitted no traffic to move . . . as in the best times in Cuzco or Quillabamba.

It may have been that the commercial bourgeois group, represented by the Cáceras family, [3] initially favored the strike. If so, they served only as a channel for it, because the strike came from the very depths of the people, the people who denounced the agrarian reform [4] as a farce perpetrated on the peasants, the people who cannot be fooled by golden lights or Popular Cooperation.[5] Yes, it is the people after the deception. It is Puno that emerges calling forth its brothers who are still sluggish. Puno who tells the officials to shut down the tribunal or be stoned. Puno who stones that symbol of the sacred cows of oligarchic justice.

They had no interest in false promises. "They burned the legislators in effigy, saying that that was a symbol of the rupture between them and the people." They made giant strides; it could be that among the effigies burned were those of the Cáceras, or it could be that as yet they weren't; in any event, the Cáceras would not be capable of holding back the exploited masses of Puno.

The rebellious people of Qolla rose up on a departmental scale, announcing new achievements, new demonstrations of popular courage on the part of the Peruvian peasants and their sister classes.

The strike was called off, the battle ended, but there has been a victory. Not because of the promises made by the government, promises that are always sold out, but because of the mobilization itself, because of the battle itself that educates, that teaches, that is the teacher of the people. The battle is over, and it is just as well that it did not continue, because the masses still do not have the leadership that their courage deserves. There is no revolutionary party on a national scale capable of leading them in great and decisive combats. The FIR is preparing itself to become that party, and calls upon the entire revolutionary left to unite for this great task.

There are the masses, comrades, *making the revolution.* Yes, we now know that they did not call for the destruction of the reactionary government and its replacement by a revolutionary one; yes, we know that they demanded something much more modest, but *it is the revolution;* we recognize it in its popular form. It is also possible that there were no leftists among the leaders, but *it is the revolution.* We recognize it in the Indians of Ayavirí, tearing up the railroad tracks. It is possible that there was no guerrilla group there, but they were the masses, yes, comrades, masses united by their repudiation of the legislature's excessive collaborationism, masses conscious that the agrarian reform law is a trick, masses who decided to fight in their way, the plebeian way: highways blockaded, stones thrown at the sacrosanct covenant of the law. *And that is the revolution.*

Yes, we know that with stones you do not topple a government; yes we know it. But the consciousness, the will, capable of throwing a stone at the oppressor, will seize the weapon needed to topple the government.

For us, the weapon is at the service of man, not the man at the service of the weapon; and when the heart and the mind are revolutionary, the hands will follow suit.

Cult of spontaneity? No! Underestimation of the techniques of struggle acquired by the people of the world in their struggle? No!

We know that without a conscious, revolutionary leadership, the struggle of the masses will not be victorious. We know that the Peruvian masses must take advantage of the knowledge, the experience, the methodology, the techniques and the tactics of the revolutionaries of the world.

But we also know that if the masses of Puno continue to follow bourgeois leaders and do not use the methodology they should use, it is not their fault but ours. The mission of the revolutionary is to go to the masses, to serve them, to put his knowledge at their disposal, at the service of the process lived by the masses, at the service of the revolutionary course that the masses follow.

It is not revolutionary to climb to the summit of the revolution with the scheme of what is "inevitable" in your hand, scorning the masses for "not supporting us," for "not following," looking with disdain at their "reformist land claims," their "low level," and their "primitive means of struggle."

The masses will not "link up with the armed struggle." No. That is putting things backwards. The armed struggle will emerge from the masses. The role of the revolutionary is to stimulate and lead this process.

The gun does not fire by itself, it takes hands as well as a will to pull the trigger. We are with the people who now handle the *warak'a* [sling] because we know that they are capable later on of taking up rifles and machine guns. And of winning.

The FIR has signed a pact with the revolutionary process in Peru, and issues a call to all the parties of the revolutionary left to endorse it.

We are indebted to revolutionary Puno, comrades. May we rise to her stature!

Puna, a Story

" . . . And then he says he was beaten with a club, and from then on he was not as he should be—sick, he walked badly. Yes, indeed, he died last year, but he has two boys, two he's got. Now in the union assembly they are surely going to tell you all about it; they know all about it, those men; with doctors, moreover, they have taken people to see doctors, one

person from here — yes, indeed — another they brought from
Ocongate. To Cuzco they took him, moreover, to the hospital,
though the hospital heads didn't want to take him. They said,
'There is no bed.' Each day thinner, also his eyes sunken,
yes, indeed. An injection they also gave him, he says. But
the injection did not make him well, none of their prescriptions
made him well. His boys know all about it; two boys he's
got, now they are going to be in the assembly."

"And his cattle?"

"Up to now they are grabbing them, I'm telling you so.
His sons still cannot get them back."

"Afraid?"

"How could it be otherwise?"

"Good, *compañero*, it's just as well that they don't try to
get them back; if they are going to be in the assembly I don't
believe they can be too fearful. The return or payment for
those cattle has to be one of the points the union will demand."

"Furthermore, Marcos Quispe has complained about his cattle to the governor, the police, and the judge — all for nothing.
Worse yet, in the police station they locked him up for twenty-
four hours; besides, the judge told him, 'Listen, Indian, this
gentleman is not a half-breed cattle thief like you, that you
should say such things; furthermore, he is very good to his
Indians, since he hasn't brought a suit against you for slander
and put you in jail.'"

"Who is the judge?"

"Eudocio Luna, the landlord of Ch'illka."

"I know that scoundrel, he has another hacienda in Anta.
So it is, *compañero*, the *gamonales* themselves are the authorities: prefects, sub-prefects, presidents, deputies, judges. And
when it's not themselves, it's their friends, their servants.

"They make the laws according to their own whims, they
force us all to obey them, and they are the first to disregard
them.

"They are respectable persons, decent folk, distinguished citizens, society, and many other such titles. If they ever enter
a jail cell, it's because they have had a falling out among
rich people, and even then, they don't go into a cell but into
a clinic.

"There is injustice throughout Peru, *compañero*, but it's worse
in the countryside, to be sure; it's more barefaced, more cruel
and brutal, more primitive; but all the poor people are made
brothers by this injustice and for that reason our struggle must
be united."

Remigio Condori listens in silence, and remains silent after

listening. Does he understand? . . . Doesn't he understand? . . .
Does he believe? . . . Doesn't he believe? . . . Is he only
chewing?

Jorje Carrión listens to Condori's silence, nothing but that
silence, and respects it, preserves it, heeds it, understands it,
lets it be; and if anyone wanted to interrupt he would defend
that silence with his blood.

There the two of them are, walking through the *puna*[1] in
that silence of Condori's and the tic-tac, tic-tac, tic-tac of their
steps, the slow, deliberate rhythm of Condori, the faster rhythm
of Carrión . . . time bomb, tic-tac, tic-tac, tic-tac.

And thus, the *puna*, time, the *puna*. . . .

Suddenly, in his silence, Carrión bends down: he has seen
an *achanqaray* — how pretty! — and he thinks of Eliana's hair —
even prettier! Eliana smiling with his *achanqaray* in her
hair. . . . And it could be . . . he would be able to bring her
the red flower on his way back. Yes, he would bring her one.
And the peasants? Would they think him foolish? No, not so,
since the peasant women and men wear flowers in their hats;
yes, he would bring her one, but . . . it would not arrive so
fresh in Cuzco. . . . Now then! He would take a whole branch
so that he could pick out the most luxuriant one.

"As red as your dreams," he would tell Eliana, but that didn't
please him much, because Eliana doesn't believe in those red
dreams. For him, they are dreams of flesh and bone, with
names, with ponchos, with the women wearing *ojotas* on their
feet, there, right before him, went one.

In T'impugh many people were waiting for him: Marcos
Quispe, the sons of Toribio Puma . . . "but he's got two boys,
two he's got," and many more. But on reaching T'impugh
the first thing he would do would be to drink some *chicha*,
or water, or whatever there was because he had a fierce thirst.
What a thirst you get on the *puna*! And why not, with this
sun! And the hills! His whole body is soaked with sweat, his
temples throb and throb; he dries his forehead on the sleeve
of his jacket — sweat; and now he is not thinking, just walking,
walking, his eyes averted — the ground, footsteps, his sleeve,
footsteps, the sun, stomp, stomp, stomp of footsteps . . . a
gentle little breeze — what a fine breeze! more, just perfect now,
fresh and good.

"Let's rest, *compañero*."

"But I'm really not tired yet; don't worry about me."

"Let's rest."

"Okay, you know the way." And he sits down on the ground
that has been beckoning him for some time now.

Condori sits down too. "Have a little coca."[2]

"Thanks."

Was it right to accept it? His temples are still pounding, but now he is thinking. Should he have accepted it? 'Coca poisons the Peruvian peasant. Coca is an instrument of *gamonalismo.*'

"Always be choosy, *compañero,* some have *llika,*[3] but that does damage."

"So I've heard."

There is no water, but with this he will forget his thirst a little and his fatigue; the coca will help him get to T'impugh. "Coca is an instrument of *gamonalismo.*" True, it is an instrument of hunger, of thirst, of exhaustion. We have to kill hunger, thirst, and exhaustion for real and not just the feeling of it as coca does; and coca too we have to kill for real, and for that reason he is going to T'impugh; his task is not to kill the feeling merely, and for that purpose he is chewing coca. Now he is thinking all this, but at the moment he took it and put it into his mouth, he wasn't thinking anything, his mind was pre-occupied by his sweating and the pounding in his temples.

Peacefulness.

A cloud! Thanks.

That Quispe is tenacious in his protest; he would be a good secretary of defense and would see his work bear fruit.

"And the governor, what did he tell Quispe?"

"'If you bring me a hen, I will not inform Señor Anselmo of what you have told me.'"

"And he gave him a hen?"

"That's how it is, *compañero.*"

Condori continued chewing solemnly. Ay! I chew coca, and it makes me remember everything.

Carrión continues thinking of Quispe; surely it was on his initiative that they organized the union.

"And are you people also thinking of organizing, *compañero?*"

"I have known, *compañero,* for a long time I have known about these questions. I know about the union, the assembly, leaders — everything. In La Convención I worked as an agricultural laborer."

"Are you a member of any union?"

"Not I, *compañero.* Well, now, I was only there a little while, you see. The tenant farmer I worked for was a member. But I attended assemblies a few times. In Quillabamba, also, I listened at meetings to all the abuse they heaped on the *gamonales,* all of it. And I always got leaflets, too; in my house

they are pasted on the wall. I showed them to everyone in
T'impugh, the children in the school can read, moreover. From
then on, I said to everyone, 'We have to get a union,' I said.
Little by little I said just that, yes indeed, but I had to be
careful of the spying *llunk'us.* 7 At the beginning, only a few
wanted to, the rest were afraid. Now most are in agreement.
'A union is good,' they say. Because the landlord's abuses
are getting worse. And so they are saying, 'to live or die,
well now, it's just the same thing,' they say, 'if we are not
going to die now, aren't we going to die later?' they say."

"It's like this, *compañero,* when we decide to struggle we
must be ready for anything. To serve the *gamonales,* the government massacres peasants who demand their rights, and
therefore we recommend that the peasants take up arms to
defend themselves."

Here Carrión pauses to study the effect of his words. He
sees no clue. But he is sure that he hasn't put his foot in it,
for it was Condori who spoke of death, and nobody is going to be so stupid as to consider dying without defending
himself. In any case, since he hasn't been able to evoke any
reaction, he wants to pursue it further.

"Does the *gamonal* carry a gun?"

"Perhaps he does, that's how it will be then; furthermore,
the landlord of Yuraqhpampa has said, 'Any Indian who
comes to me about unions I will shoot like a dog.'"

Carrión relaxes, it appears that over here the landlords
show their true colors. That is always better, it simplifies
matters.

"Should we get going, *compañero*?"

"Let's go."

Once again, the immense *puna,* steeped in pain and love.
But now neither of the two thinks along those lines, their si-
lences are of a different sort.

Condori had made the arrangements beforehand. Will the
companeros have carried out the preparations? The table must
be Máximo Yupanqui's, it is bigger even than Bonifacio's.
Martín Challco has two crystal glasses, Tomás, porcelain
plates; Juan Quispe will bring metal spoons, they have enough
metal spoons. As for the hen, there is no problem, he will
provide it. Perhaps it is not a fitting occasion to eat chicken?
Certainly others will also invite him. Hah! What will the landlord say when his *llunk'us* informs him: "Remigio Condori
brought him, he himself lodged him at his house, and he is
undoubtedly going to have a post on their executive committee." Let the *gamonal* know it now! But the *gamonal* knew

Peasant union demonstration. Banner carries the slogans "Tierra o Muerte" and "Venceremos" ["Land or Death" and "We Will Win!"]

Women's brigade in the same demonstration

The *puna*

even before, and that is why he wanted to throw him out: "Listen, you Indian beggar, you are having a bad influence on my people."

They arrive at the valley, and Condori points to a little hut far off, at the foot of a huge stone, an immense rock.

"In that house we are going to hold an assembly, *compañero*. It is a good distance from the manor house."

Carrión sees some dots in front of the hut, people are already gathering, they must be the ones who live far off; the others will see them descend into the valley and will arrive before them at the meeting place at the foot of the *wank'a,* the huge, friendly rock.

Why does one associate stones with coldness and insensibility? Surely these rocks on the *puna* make you want to hug them hard to your chest, enter them, merge yourself in them, cell by cell, and have your blood circulate through them, seeking their hearts, to find out, to learn, to understand as many things about the *puna* as they must surely know. Why this heavy weight on the *puna*? Why the cactus that is born here and dies here without ever multiplying? Could it be the "fruits of sorrow?" Why do the little flowers hug the earth? Where are the tears of this pain? Why are the sighs so deep inside that they cannot escape? Was silence born here? . . . *puna* . . . have you brought up all the pain and love from deep down, *puna,* condensed it and concentrated it? What will it be for? Surely the rock knows, it must know everything. If it obviously is calling out, if it obviously is expressing love, why do they say "like a stone?" It must be other stones!

Yes, and at the foot of this rock, heart of the *puna,* will be the assembly. What things will he hear?

From the herdsman:

"Since my ancestors, we are his herdsmen, and he has never paid us. 'You do not pay *yerbaje,** and you have a potato farm; that's your payment,' he says. When a cow breaks through the fence, we have to give him another; when cattle thieves steal them, same thing; when the *puna* takes a calf, same thing. My little girl died gathering the cows during a hurricane; they are not like sheep that group together by themselves, the cows run away frightened in all directions. My little girl caught a chill and died. He's always dissatisfied with his cheeses too: 'That's too little, you thieving Indian, I'm sure you are selling it on the side,' he says. When we draw more milk, then he complains, 'The calves are getting

---

*A tax in livestock or money which the peasants must pay the landlord for the use of pasture lands [H. B.].

too thin.' He's never satisfied. 'You are living off my cows, yes indeed, you lazy Indian,' he says. When I want to quit being his herdsman, he won't consent. 'First you have to pay me what you owe me; you owe me plenty of cows,' he says."

From others:

"He stole my cattle, too."

"Four days each week we have to work in return for the little patch of ground he lets me use."

"And there is the *pongo*." *

"And *mit'ani*." **

"Enough land he owns for all of Cuzco."

"Overtime work on the roads and during the drought isn't credited against the work time we have to put in for the hacienda. 'Overtime isn't counted,' he says."

"And he won't let us collect brushwood either, we have nothing to cook with. 'It's not public property, it belongs to the hacienda,' he says."

"He also had a child by Aquilina Huamán which he won't recognize."

"And he beat Hermenegildo Pauqar with a whip."

And many more pearls that really sum up the honorable and dignified refinement always mentioned in the accounts of the banquets and funerals of the good families that fill the society pages.

Carrión has lost respect for the morality, chivalry, and dignity of the past, the good old days, and he has shortened their names — he calls them "shit." He is proud to belong to a generation that is horrified not by miniskirts but by the whip. A generation that is smashing the principle of authority — of the authority of Señor Anselmo, Eudocio Luna, and others of their ilk.

The little dots have grown bigger, and have differentiated into men's ponchos and women's *llijllas*. [10] The *puna* has taken on the smell of people. The barking of the dogs has turned into tail-wagging around the two approaching travelers and those now hurrying to overtake them.

Looks and words much more cordial than the gentle embraces. It's them! Yes. Most beloved *compañeros,* masters of the future, determined to take charge of it, fighters born in sorrow and pain, hope of the human race. Transformers of the world.

---

* Domestic labor in the landlord's house required of the peasants [H. B.].

** Domestic labor in the landlord's house required of the peasant women, similar to the *pongo* [H. B.].

From the newly arrived group, one, infused with the collective emotion flowing from those before him, begins to speak; an elderly man offers him his age-old anguish; a mother her infinite love; a child, his optimism; a youth, his fortitude; he greets many others, and from his chest rises the word:

"*Compañerokuna!*" [*Compañeros!*]

Everyone present hears it, but the word echoes. It breaks against the great rock and scatters through the air, like stars, like wheat. It falls on the manor house, and the toad within shudders with terror; it falls on Yuraqhpampa and Ch'illka and through the coppery skin to the heart. It falls in Puno, Piura, Vietnam, the Congo, Harlem.

"*Compañerokuna!*"

Like stars, like wheat.

1967

Letter to a Peasant Leader

El Frontón Penal Colony
January 1969

Comrade:

I have read your letter with great care. I salute you, in the first place, for your interest in our peasant brothers, and in the second place, for the clarity with which you grasp the problems. I will try to answer you.

Above all, we must always keep in mind that the historic problem of the peasant, around which all others revolve, is the problem of the *land.* Another thing we must never forget is that your struggle is only a part of the struggle of the exploited against the exploiters, and that the road to solving all the problems of the peasantry is to seize the political power from the hands of the exploiters and form a workers' and peasants' government.

Nothing short of this will fully solve the problems of the peasantry. Therefore, in all the efforts we make to win small victories, we must not lose sight of the fact that these victories represent only a step forward in our liberation struggle.

It might seem strange that we, who affirm that only with the seizure of state power by the workers will their problems be definitively solved, are also the ones who attribute the greatest importance to each victory won by the workers, however small it may be.

We consider each success a step forward, mainly because the *way* it has been achieved educates the peasantry, especially when it has a well-tested revolutionary leadership. We gain each victory, no matter how small it may be, through the collective and militant action of the peasantry. At all times we recommend collective action, unity of action, and after each success we show how it resulted from this mass action.

We always show that the authorities are the class enemies of the peasants, and that if they have made some concession, it is not because of their "sense of justice" but because of their fear of the wrath of the masses and in order to coopt them precisely by making them believe that they are "just authorities."

The best thing we gain from each victory, aside from the victory itself, is the *lesson* for the masses. Each triumph serves to give them more confidence in themselves, in the power of their united action. Each triumph serves to show them that we are in a war of exploited against exploiters. With this criterion, even defeats can be educational.

We function this way because we are profoundly convinced that only through their own actions will the workers be able to free themselves, and that therefore it is most important that they have confidence in their own ability and that they learn how to fight. When we accomplish this, we will have accomplished everything.

For this reason, those leaders who attribute victories to the sense of justice of some official or to the cleverness of a lawyer or to their own ability, we consider dangerous traitors. Although we do not totally disregard such factors, we must constantly make clear that the fundamental force is the workers' fighting unity. Sometimes we win a victory without carrying out any act of force. That is because even the suggestion, even the possibility of forceful action intimidates the enemy.

I consider, comrade, that these general principles will serve you in your future struggle better than a thousand bits of detailed advice that I might give you. Nevertheless, while I can, I will continue collaborating with you with all my strength.

Let us move on to the concrete matter. There are five demands that you raise:

1. Return of stolen lands
2. Abolition of the abuses by the "distinguished citizens" or *llaqhta taytas*
3. Purchase of a hacienda
4. A school
5. Abolition of the *yerbaje* in money, in kind, or in labor

We see that all this can be solved by only one measure:

the first thing that should be done is to form a union of tenants and freeholders.

The point is that the first step has to be the formation of one single union to which the tenant farmers from various haciendas and the members of various communal villages will belong: a union with doors that are open to all peasants. Later on, when it is stronger, we will see if committees evolve for each hacienda or communal village, or if several unions evolve and are grouped in a district federation. For now, I believe it is necessary to concentrate your forces and form one single union.

This union will be the body that decides what to do with respect to the land problem. For my part, I think that the purchase of that hacienda is a mistake; not only because the land belongs to the peasant, and he has no reason to pay a cent for it, but also, chiefly, because it fosters divisions among the peasants and thereby weakens your movement and strengthens the enemy. That is the bitter lesson we learned in Ongoy, and in many other cases, when the "buyers" went over to the side of the enemy against their brothers.

You too will understand what happens when some have money and others do not; some have more and others less; and when the landlord proposes a price, those most readily disposed to accept it will be those who have the most money. There may be some who buy larger tracts than others, become little *gamonales*. In summary, I feel that the purchase, whether direct or through the intermediary of the famous agrarian reform, would be a step backward, not forward. In any event, the decision must be made by the majority of the peasant masses, when they are organized.

The other points must indeed be raised. Almost from the beginning of the organization you will begin to weaken the abuses of the big shots, partly through the fear that they will begin to feel and partly because the peasants will begin to feel strong. Something similar is going to happen with respect to the abuses of the *yerbaje;* they are going to begin disappearing right from the start.

Nevertheless, the fundamental problem is going to remain the *land.* We must encourage the reclamation of the stolen lands and fight little by little for the total liquidation of the *yerbaje;* even though at the beginning we are only demanding that they return to the community the land which has clearly been stolen, we will not cease our struggle until we have put an end to *gamonalismo* and succeeded in taking ownership of the land for those who work it.

Returning to the matter of the *yerbaje:* I believe that the first thing that we must demand is that, since we now pay in money, we shouldn't have to work a single day to pay for the *yerbaje,* nor be forced to sell them cattle. We can also demand a decrease in the amount of the *yerbaje.* All this depends on how strong we are.

On the subject of the school: it will be the union that will demand its construction. If we win, it will be a victory for the peasant movement. If we don't, it will be additional proof to expose the bourgeois government's indifference to peasant education. In any event, when the peasants have the land in their hands, they will be able to afford a school, and much more besides. (Our union in Chaupimayo negotiated for a school for years, without results. After we took the land into our own hands, we ourselves built and paid for the school; now the government has voluntarily financed the school and is maintaining it, even though nobody asked them, as part of their plan to coopt the peasant struggle.) In summary: to this and other demands, the government will respond more or less according to the degree of our strength.

I think that we have now dealt with the five points. Let's pass now to the subject of the formation of the union. I believe that twenty peasants is a reasonable number to start with.

With respect to achieving recognition, keep in mind that sometimes the government refuses to recognize a group, even if it is a mass organization. For example, it issued a special decree denying the peasants of La Convención the right to unionize, and only our strength forced them to retract it.

On the whole legal aspect, it is necessary to consult a legal advisor who is familiar with peasant matters. The party will know whom to recommend. It is always necessary to remember that the legal advisor is just that: a legal advisor. He is not called upon to play the role of union leader or political leader. For the former, there are union leaders; for the latter, there is a revolutionary vanguard of the workers: the FIR. We consult him because he is a legal advisor.

In order for the exploiting class to exercise its domination, it has provided itself with laws, judges, etc., that serve the double purpose of guaranteeing its domination and tricking the workers into believing that there is justice, that laws exist that protect them under the bourgeois regime, and that therefore they need not move against that regime to defend their rights.

To maintain this deception, they have laws that "protect" the workers, and at times they feel obliged to make concessions to the workers' demands. That is why the constitution recognizes the right of association, forbids unpaid labor, and so forth.

Since the unions are weak at first, they are obliged to ask only that the laws be enforced. Nevertheless, because the *gamonales* do not obey even their own laws, to win this enforcement even in part is a triumph. In any case, we should never cease demonstrating to the workers that "the authorities are enforcing this law only because we are strong"; "this abuse is stopping not because our lawyer has invoked a law correctly, nor because that law exists, nor because the authorities are just, but because of our strength, because of what we have done and because they are afraid of what we may do." From the beginning, I repeat, we need the legal advisor very much, because we will be obliged by our weakness to confine our action within the framework of the law.

Nevertheless, little by little, the peasantry will become more and more convinced that winning one or another victory doesn't depend on whether there is a law, that this is a minor factor. The peasants will realize that those victories are due to their own strength and will understand as a result that they have no reason to confine their demands within the framework of bourgeois law, the law of the *gamonales*. Then their task is to topple the capitalists and the *gamonales* along with their laws, their codes and their judges; to destroy all of that by their own strength, the strength that has brought their victories.

But for all this to come about, you have to begin at the beginning.

With respect to organizing the union: once you have gathered together a set number of peasants and they agree to organize a union, proceed to the election of the executive committee. It can be four members, ten, twenty, or whatever, depending on the number of peasants who are in the union.

All this is very flexible; it is best if you take what I say only as an illustration. If there are twenty peasants, I believe that an executive committee of four is enough, and if there are one hundred, it can be ten or fifteen. Let us see what the principal responsibilities are:

Secretary-General— He is the central leader who coordinates the action of the entire leadership; he is the one who represents the union. The most important qualification for this and for all other positions is not the ability to read, nor how many years of school he has had, but his militancy, spirit of self-sacrifice, his interest in discharging the duties of this office, his dynamism.

Secretary of Defense— His title describes his job: to take charge of everything that relates to defense; this means concern over any abuse of an individual member as well as the general defense of the union. In the early stages, his work is closely related to the land claims, to facing the authorities, and to working with the lawyer. Later, perhaps, he will be charged with organizing armed militias. For the present his job is more "legal."

Financial Secretary— This is the treasurer. He is charged with collecting dues, controlling expenses, and busying himself in general with the finances of the union.

Organizational Secretary— Handles membership, convokes assemblies, meetings, etc.

Recording Secretary— Keeps the minutes of the meetings and keeps track of publications and documents that may be of interest.

(The student comrades will be able to explain to you about other officers: for cooperatives, for press and propaganda, for external relations, etc. They have almost the same functions as in the trade unions.)

Secretary of Culture— In charge of everything that relates to the school, to education, etc.

You can have a secretary of public works, a secretary of agrarian reform, a secretary of the women's front, etc.

Secretary of Discipline— Has the function of judge. The peasant must not go to the bourgeois judges to settle internal problems. This secretary can have a set of standards for cases involving damages caused by animals who get into someone else's fields, and whatever other problems of this sort may arise.

(All this, I repeat, is very flexible. You can figure out how many positions, and which ones, you need. When there are many members, you will need subsecretaries who will work closely with the secretaries.)

Cooperatives— The exploiters and their servants like to talk about cooperatives because they see in this a way of distracting the peasants' attention from the main subject: the land. By talking about cooperatives they want to make us believe that the peasants' problems can be solved without destroying *gamonalismo* and capitalism.

It is the duty of the unions to clear this deception out of the peasants' heads, to explain to them that the cooperative is only one of the functions of the union. The revolutionary leadership must explain that a socialist country would be the best type of cooperative for all the workers of the countryside and city, that if Peru is really going to belong to them all collectively, they will first have to sweep away the oppressors.

Land or Death! We Will Win!   Hugo Blanco G.

Simon Oviedo

He was born beside a deep river, in one of those regions that they say produce only gentle people.

He was born on the banks of the Apurímacc; what wise words could this river have murmured to him?

He was born in Pillpinto, the land of the butterflies, but he could not play very long with them; he had to work, work, work. He had to turn a little plot of communal land into bread, a plot smaller than his father's had been, smaller still than his grandfather's had been; such is the land of the *ayllus,* it shrinks and shrinks; and the people multiply and multiply. In Pillpinto there was a school, but Simón could not attend — he had to work, work, work.

His children, now, can already read: Chaupimayo and Oviedo have given them a school. Chaupimayo and Oviedo have told them that they must go to school, and also play.

He loved his land very much, he loved the river of soft, wise words, and the butterflies; but there was not enough land for him to live in Pillpinto; there was not enough land for many Pillpinteños, and for that reason there are Pillpinteños all over the place: they are in the slums of Lima, selling trinkets in the little villages in the sierra, they are selling their strength all over.

Like all free men — for the Peruvians are free — Simón had to make a choice: he could freely choose the place where he would be exploited. He chose a climate very similar to the climate of his home, Chaupimayo. And he chose a master: Alfredo Romainville.

From that moment on, his history is the history of Chaupimayo, and that is no small thing.

He was a timid beast of burden that trembled under the whip of his master.

When the rebel winds blew, when Andrés Gonzáles uttered his cry, flung out his challenge: Unionize! Simón Oviedo was there. And it was not just any union. It was a union started because of Romainville; it was a union born of the struggle with the Aprista traitors.

Chaupimayo and Oviedo, Oviedo and Chaupimayo, one and the same, the same militancy springing from the same humiliation.

Chaupimayo and Oviedo, crossing the hills to confront the bullets of the *gamonales* in Amaybamba and Huyro and to seize the weapon that would be wielded by the Indian.

Chaupimayo and Oviedo organizing revolutionary unions.

Chaupimayo and Oviedo crossing the hills to pull Fortunato Vargas out of prison in Santa María, for Vargas was a brother of Pillpinto, a brother of Chaupimayo, a brother in the struggle.

Chaupimayo and Oviedo crossing the hills throughout the entire night; fighting fatigue, fighting sleep, fighting the Civil Guards; traveling by night until they reach the highway, and then stopping and searching every car that passes to discover which one holds Hugo Blanco, their brother, prisoner; to snatch him from the enemy's grasp, and to return him to his own people, revolutionary Chaupimayo.

Oviedo and Chaupimayo in Cuzco, on a hunger strike to stir up the department and free Leonidas Carpio, Fortunato Vargas, and Carrión from the central jail, since this time Chaupimayo couldn't do it alone.

Chaupimayo and Oviedo on countless other journeys.

Chaupimayo and Oviedo produce the guerrilla band, but Oviedo himself cannot be in it because he has an infected foot.

The guerrillas, the Remigio Huamán Peasant Union Brigade, snipe away at the enemy; the enemy cannot find them because they are hidden in the bosom of their people, the organized peasant masses.

The wild beast grows desperate, the assault guard vents its fury on Chaupimayo; the executioners grab a woman comrade and beat her face with their rifle butts. They are armed to the teeth, and there are many of them. They are terrible beasts. No rational man would think of confronting them in those circumstances. But Oviedo is not a rational man, he is the fury of his people, exploited since the beginning of time.

"Imapunitaqh kasqankichisri!" [What foul monsters you are!] And he hurls himself against the rifles with his iron tool held aloft, his iron tool turned into a weapon, turned into his fury.

The animals fired flashes of light, and the iron tool sliced the air. Oviedo falls shouting, the bullets continue tearing at him.

His blood irrigates all of Chaupimayo, the repressive forces continue smashing La Convención, the FIR is destroyed, and the leftists continue discussing what Chaupimayo should do. A peace of the sword is imposed. Traitorous bureaucrats, products of the repression and of "peace," are imposed on La Convención. They forget about Oviedo, they never mention him — he represents the struggle.

But his people remember him, his people know that his iron tool-weapon has not merely sliced the air, but that Simón did that to sharpen it, so that it would be able to cut off the head of the monster.

We will cut it off, Simón, the FIR promises you; we will cut it off, little brother.

1969

Students: To the Countryside!

El Frontón Penal Colony
August 1969

The Peruvian peasantry has demonstrated throughout its history that when it rises up to fight for its rights, not even death will stand in its way.

It has also demonstrated that it is capable of organizing and systematizing its struggle, multiplying its forces enormously.

In addition, it has been demonstrated that the unity of consciously revolutionary students with the peasant forces produces positive results.

As a peasant union leader of university origins, as a member of the peasant guerrilla group of La Convención, which arose from the maturity of the organized peasants' experience, I exhort the university students to fulfill their historic duty in this hour: *to the countryside en masse* under the coordination of your own organizations.

The hour has arrived for the university students to demonstrate that they are not the windbags of the Peruvian revolution, but its activists. The hour has arrived to demonstrate that their confidence in the peasantry, their confidence in the revolutionary mobilization of the peasantry, are not mere words.

The government has passed a bourgeois agrarian reform law with the object of saving the system and aiding the capitalist development of the country for the benefit of the national bourgeois and imperialist sectors. The government says that this law for the purchase and sale of the land will end the exploitation that the peasantry has suffered for centuries. The government uses the slogan, "Peasant, the landlord will no longer grow fat on your poverty." The government says that it counts on the support of the peasants, workers, and students.

We, the revolutionaries, defend the two basic principles of the agrarian reform law decreed and put into effect by the peasant movement of La Convención in 1962:

1. That the land pass into the hands of the peasants with no compensation to the landlords.

2. That the organizations carrying out the agrarian reform be agrarian reform committees democratically elected by the peasant organizations.

We, the revolutionaries, know that the real agrarian reform will not reward the landlord with a payment wrung from the poverty of the peasant, as this law attempts to do.

We, the revolutionaries, know that the peasant and the country more than ever before need to use this money for the cultivation of the soil.

We, the revolutionaries, know that the correct form of the agrarian reform is "Land, Yes — Payment, No."

We, the revolutionaries, do not even have any confidence that this bourgeois law will be put into effect by the bureaucracy. We know that ever since colonial times they have been enacting laws that benefit the peasant but never enforce them. We know that lack of enforcement follows normally under this government. Normally, too, will criminal *gamonalismo* continue, as the crimes of the repressive forces continue.

We know that the *gamonalismo* has bought and continues to buy all types of authorities and functionaries. We know that in this way it bought the functionaries of the agrarian reform of the last regime, and there is no reason to believe it will act differently under the present regime.

We, the revolutionaries, know that under the previous regime, and under the present regime, in the name of agrarian reform, they are trying to force the peasantry of La Convención to pay for lands obtained through its reclamation struggle, and that by democratic decision of the mass conventions, those lands belong to the peasants. We know that the authorities are trying to make the communal villagers pay for land that is rightfully theirs, and that was partially regained by their struggle against the repressive forces from the hands of the Cerro de Pasco Copper Corporation and other thieving firms; these communal lands, even according to the bourgeois laws, are the inalienable property of the communal villages.

We, the revolutionaries, know that only the organized mobilization of the peasantry against *gamonalismo* and its accomplices will be able to accomplish an authentic agrarian reform. We know that in that way it will become the agrarian revolution, as part of the process of the socialist revolution led by the proletariat.

For all these reasons, the revolutionary students must flock to the countryside, to spark the organization of the peasantry.

It must be the organized peasantry that decides who has the right to take action on the agrarian reform law.

The government says that it has confidence in the peasantry. We, the revolutionaries, have profound confidence in the peasantry. Let it be the peasants who decide. Let us encourage their organization so that they will do so.

With regard to the university students' problems: never will they be resolved within the capitalist system. The government that has passed a law restricting the rights of university students is the same government that purports to be carrying out an agrarian reform. Therefore, the best way to fight for student demands at this time is to flock to the countryside to move that powerful revolutionary force: the peasantry.

I hope that the Peruvian students know how to rise to the heights of the mission that history is offering them at this time. We consider the students who go to the countryside to be authentic revolutionaries, even if they now sincerely believe in this government, in this law, and go to help its enforcement. They are truly interested in their peasant brothers, and therefore they go to the countryside. Contact with reality will show them who is right.

It doesn't make you a revolutionary to talk and talk about agrarian reform; to talk about it only, whatever position you defend, however revolutionary it may be, remains mere talk as long as you do not leave the city.

The agrarian reform, the agrarian revolution, will not be made from the school desk, but from the countryside.

Students: To the Countryside!
Land or Death! We Will Win!

Hugo Blanco G.

The Peasant Movement

El Frontón Penal Colony
August 20, 1969

Throughout our history, the peasant movements in Peru have had, and have at present, the land as their fundamental objective. It is for this reason that the revolutionary slogan *Land or Death!* has become the staple of the peasant vanguard.

The most recent mobilizations do not contradict this. In Cospán and Huancaya, this is clearly the aim; they fight to recover the land. As the Huanta, we know that there the basis of the student and democratic movements was the great problem of the land. For years, the peasantry suffered the robbery of its lands by the *gamonales* of the zone and, as a result of peasant reclamations, the authorities unleashed a legal repression without concealing their pro-*gamonal* bias. The events at Ayacucho related to the student problem were the last straw, and the peasantry exploded.

The previous agrarian reform law, accompanied by Popular Cooperation, had succeeded in bridling the upsurge of the peasant impetus, filling them with illusions; but soon they became disillusioned and began a new awakening.

Now this present reformist junta passes a new law, more advanced than the previous one, although in essence it too is a law providing for the purchase and sale of the land. It is possible that they will really try to apply it, for it aims not only to bridle the peasant movement but also — reflecting the interests of the pro-development bourgeois sectors, national as well as imperialist — it tries, on one hand, to create an internal market of small proprietors, consumers of industrial commodities; and on the other, to provide funds for capitalist industrial development.

We repeat that because of these bourgeois desires, it is possible that the government will try to apply the law. But the desires of the junta will not be enough to apply this law. There are other factors.

On one hand there are the *gamonales,* who have always bought officials, thus evading the application of any laws that work against their absolute domination. The bureaucracy — that is, the authorities and the functionaries — will remain just as corrupt as before. Bribes will be on the order of the day. The industrial haciendas on the coast — the strongholds of the old oligarchy, like ancient feudal castles — from which they fought to the bitter end against any move for economic development, are one thing. (On expropriating these haciendas, the junta liquidated all trace of APRA's influence on the workers of this zone.) It is another thing to talk about the widely separated holdings of the *gamonales* of the sierra who, if they have less influence on a national scale than the sugar and cotton magnates, are nevertheless masters locally.

Not that they are going to oppose the agrarian reform law by force, much less will they organize armed resistance. They are going to do the same as always: bribe the authorities and functionaries to delay and distort the application of even this bourgeois law.

And the bureaucracy remains the bureaucracy: in addition

to fulfilling its function of serving the oppressors (in this case the pro-development bourgeois sector), it more than ever serves its own interests. It will certainly offer no resistance to bribery.

On the other hand, there is the peasantry, which in many instances will oppose the application of the law, and will almost always oppose the way in which it is being applied.

From all these contradictions, the most likely outcome is that some distorted, sluggish, highly bureaucratized application of the law will result in the interior of the country.

In this whole process, there will be bloody conflicts and skirmishes. But we do not deceive ourselves: the contradictions between the junta and the *gamonales* will not lead to skirmishes. The bloody conflicts will not be between them, for a *gamonal* would have to be very stupid not to give in to the government in the final instance.

The struggles will be as always: on one hand, the peasantry, in defense of its rights and for the land, against the abuses of the *gamonales,* against the bias of the authorities; on the other hand, the repressive forces in defense of the exploiters, whether they be the *gamonales* of the zone or all the exploiters jointly represented by the junta.

Until now, the struggles have been "spontaneous." But there is another factor, the political vanguard, the revolutionaries who are going to the masses, to root themselves in those "spontaneous" organizations, to listen to and assess the "spontaneous" aspirations, and to participate in the peasants' "spontaneous" struggles. From there, from the very center of the real, existing peasant movement, with the heart of Túpac Amaru in our chest, with the blood of our martyrs pulsing through our veins, we will guide the struggle, we will organize it, we will lead it to the agrarian revolution as a part of the socialist revolution headed by the proletariat. The fundamental slogans of the FIR for the countryside continue to be the same: Organization, extension and coordination of the peasant movement.

And what about the law? Our principled position is firm: this bourgeois law for purchasing land, entrusted to the bureaucrats for enforcement, is not what the FIR calls for. The Trotskyists have defended, and we do defend, the slogan: Land, Yes — Payment, No. Let committees elected by the peasantry administer the agrarian reform. We have defended this, and we have practiced it in La Convención.

Nevertheless, we have always respected and paid attention to the desires of the workers. If there are peasant sectors that want this bourgeois law applied, we will fight with them to get it applied, watching to see that all its positive aspects are carried out, and fighting against all the negative aspects. We shall always insist that only the mobilization of the peasantry can be the guarantee for even this limited bourgeois law. We shall always insist on the organization, extension, and coordination of the peasant movement. And we shall insist on the peasantry's direct participation in the administration of the law.

In La Convención, our active and militant position is clear: We will not pay one cent to the enemy! The land is ours, we have won it with our struggle, with the blood of our martyrs, with the tortures and imprisonment suffered by our leaders!

Now that the land is in our hands, now that the peasantry has made its own agrarian reform, what is needed is to defend it and to spread the process, not independently but tied to the struggle of the entire peasantry and the people in general.

Another important issue relates to the huge tracts of land throughout Peru that have been seized illegally from the peasant villages, seized illegally even by bourgeois standards. The *gamonales* are going to try to avoid returning those lands to their legitimate owners by means of the agrarian reform law, claiming that those lands are being expropriated and that they must be paid for. In such cases we must fight for the plain and simple return of those lands.

With regard to the question of the organization of the masses, we must be quite flexible. We have always preferred the union as the form of mass organization for the peasantry; until now it has shown itself to be the most appropriate form for the struggle. Nevertheless, we must not make a fetish of the union. If the peasants respect their communal organization and can utilize it for their struggle, we have no reason to insist that they organize a union. The struggle of the communal villagers in the central part of the country shows us that. In Ongoy, on the other hand, the peasant association was the combat group, in opposition to the antiquated and bureaucratized communal organization.

Regarding the cooperatives that the law calls for: if the peasants are organized democratically in unions, village communes, etc., we will fight to get the cooperative into the hands of their organization. Even if such an organization does not exist, we will fight to form one, for its goals are broad, and the cooperative would only be one of its functions. But if the peasants have already entered in a massive way into the cooperative proposed by the government and consider it their own organization, then we will fight inside it, as much to make it thoroughly democratic as to see that it broadens its field of activity.

Finally, the details in specific working outline cannot be determined beforehand, but will be a product of direct contact with the reality, and any attempt to detail a plan of action a priori would only result in hollow words; the revolutionaries who go to the countryside and join the peasant movement will be those, in short, who will tell us what must be done. The form of struggle depends on reality, and the reality of the countryside is in the countryside. This redundant statement is necessary because there are many people who imagine that the countryside is in the classroom.

The last agrarian reform law alleviated some of the tension in the countryside, decreasing thereby the possibility of armed struggle. Nevertheless, the contradictions did not disappear, and others arose. The development of these new conflicts toward armed struggle depends on the incorporation of the revolutionaries into the life of the current peasant movement, beginning with its present organizations, its present consciousness and present necessities, its concrete, immediate, and most deeply felt demands, and the sooner they join and participate in these the sooner will they consciously be able to transform this struggle from its present low level to armed struggle.

And in armed struggle, as in other stages of the struggle — and even more so than in other stages because it follows them — only contact with reality will be able to indicate to us specifically how the armed struggle must develop, what organizational forms it will take, for instance. Meanwhile, we keep our demand for union defense brigades, and they arise out of the very thick of the struggle. More concrete details in this respect, a priori plans that claim to lead to victory, are the domain of armchair theorists.

We, the Trotskyists, must listen to the revolutionaries who speak to us from the countryside, from within the peasant movement. The forecasts made by them are the ones we respect most. This is all the more so now that there are so many windbags about armed struggle, who don't even know where the countryside is.

We know that the peasants will fight with weapons in hand for the revolution; but at present, in Peru, the proletariat acquires greater importance each day as the vanguard par excellence of the socialist revolution. We have seen such important manifestations of the class struggle in the cities that we cannot even affirm in general terms that the revolution in Peru will begin first in the countryside. The proletariat commands more respect each day, and it could be that it will decide to assume from the outset the vanguard role that history has indicated for it.

Regarding the debate among students about the usefulness of a massive migration to the countryside on the occasion of the enactment of this agrarian reform law, our position is the following:

We repeat our call to university students to go in massive numbers to the countryside. We maintain our criticism of the agrarian reform, but we do not hang around the cities to discuss it. It is more revolutionary to go to the countryside to promote this law, sincerely believing in it, than to stay at the university to oppose it from the revolutionary position solely in "scientific" argument.

The revolutionary position on the agrarian reform needs to be upheld in action. The position of the FIR is clear on this question: Students to the countryside, working through your own organizations!

It is precisely in the course of all this work, and within that movement, that it is essential to build the party organization in the countryside, with the best elements who have emerged in the class struggle. This was the fundamental shortcoming in La Convención, the deficiency which generated all the others. The syndicalism for which we criticized ourselves with respect to Chaupimayo didn't consist in failing to raise the economic demands of the masses to the political plane — this was done, and in general it was done correctly. Our syndicalism was rooted in our failure to crystallize that political advance of the masses, and especially of the vanguard, in a political organization with Bolshevik discipline that would consolidate the best of that vanguard.

Even the unification of the revolutionary left itself will come about in the course of this work, just as it will come about in the course of work in the cities, mainly among the working class, starting also from its present struggles; thus, through a program of transitional demands, we will arrive at the socialist revolution.

Land or Death! We Will Win!

Hugo Blanco G.

The Teacher, a Story

What follows is an excerpt from my last letter to José María Arguedas,[1] the very great Indian writer. The letter was written in Quechua, November 25, 1969, four days before the bullet that put an end to his life. The letter was received but not read, or read only in part. [H. B.]

So that you may see that my roots are those of a common man, roots grown in our own soil, I send you this story that I am writing about my friend, don Lorenzo. It is not fiction, my friend. I am telling what really happened, even the names are true.

For some time, I have wanted to tell about this great man, so that everyone could see the strength of our Indian roots. I lacked only the time to do it; but now, hearing that you were sick, I said "For once, I'm going to do it, to send it to my friend José María, so that at least he will have this to comfort him while he is ill, so he will be comforted with our sad joy." Saying this, my friend, I did it quickly, and now I am sending it to you with all my heart.

The stewed leaves of the mustard tree we call *nabos hauch'a*. We like them a lot, in spite of their evocation of death in its most silent and protracted form: starvation.

When the hunger comes, it devours the beans, corn, potatoes, and *chuño;*[2] it leaves nothing for the Indian . . . except the leaves of the mustard tree, without butter, without onions, without garlic, without even salt.

After many of these leaves comes death; they are its "green heralds." Death comes under different aliases in Spanish and Quechua: tuberculosis, pernicious anemia, pneumonia, *pujiu* (spring), *wayra* (winter), *layqa* (witchcraft). They call it by its aliases because its real name is an ugly word: starvation.

But the *nabos hauch'a* are not to blame for this; and it's for that reason that we like them so much. I don't say that they are rich, I don't understand these things. I was already mistaken about the *chuño;* I said it was very rich, and the people who know say that it is tasteless. Therefore, I only say that we like it a lot, although it reminds us of the famines.

During those famines, the *gringos* (they are so kind!) sometimes send us as charity maize with wood lice and powdered "milk" which is delivered to the church, city hall, or government office; and from there is fed to the landowners' hogs.

I don't ask that they distribute that charity to us; I ask that they return to us what is ours, so that there will be no famines. It was my first cousin, Zenón Galdos, who asked them to distribute it; it cost him dearly—for asking that, Señor Araujo, the mayor of Huanoquite, shot him dead with one bullet. Señor Araujo was not arrested; he is from a good family.

One Sunday, in nineteen hundred forty-something, while I was savoring my ration of *nabos hauch'a,* I was talking with the woman who was selling them, seated in the mud of the San Jerónimo market in Cuzco. We discussed the topic of the day: the earthquake tremors. She explained their origin to me: they were sent as a punishment because the Indians of the *ayllu* rose up against the Dominican Fathers of the Pata-pata hacienda. That was how the priest had explained the tremors at mass that very morning: "The devil has not died, he is in the hospital in Cuzco." The priest didn't say that the death of the devil was the condition for stopping the tremors, but the woman understood that from his story.

"Will he die?"

"Surely, he is very bad, they say all this is his fault."

She feared tremors, but she did not want to go to hell, and for that reason her words condemned the devil.

But her face, her voice, the mud in which she was sitting, the *nabos hauch'a,* her heart—all these were of the land, of the land, like the "devil" in the hospital, of the land that silently cried out its desperate wish to save the devil.

And Lorenzo Chamorro was saved, yes, indeed. . . . He was saved partly because he remained an invalid. The doctor told him: "Only an Indian like you could live with six holes in your belly; what's bothering you is that one of the bullets hit your spinal cord."

And so I got to know him somewhat later, still in his corner: eyes watering, grimy, with crutches, a big poncho, a vibrant voice, eyes of fire.

I looked at him and I knew that it was true that he produced tremors: my blood trembled, my knees trembled, when I went to embrace him.

"*Tayta,*[3] tell me."

And he told me things I already knew: that the Dominicans of the Pata-pata hacienda were continuing to take lands from the communal village; that the village had ownership titles; that the officials refused to do anything; that the peasants organized a union; that he was the secretary-general; that the

Dominicans had tried bribery, but he wouldn't give in; they had threatened, but the union wouldn't give up. And then, when they were working on the disputed lands, the prior of the Convent of Santo Domingo came with his thugs; and since the thugs didn't know him, the prior had pointed to him "with the same hand that consecrates the Holy Sacrament"; and then one of the thugs shot him.

"All my comrades ran to help me; I told them: 'No! Let me alone! Grab *him!* Let me alone! Let me alone! Get him!' And just then, I fainted!"

There is no jail for those who shoot Indians, nor any compensation for wounded Indians; that goes without saying; we are in Peru.

The peasants were afraid to visit him in his invalid's corner. It was dangerous . . . compromising . . . but the women went "just to see his wife," until the priest learned about it and was obliged to explain from the pulpit:

"My children, the Lord has pardoned this town, but you are abusing His kindness, your wives continue to visit the house of the devil. A rain of fire is going to fall on San Jerónimo!"

The women feared the rain of fire, and stopped going to see Chamorro's wife.

"My older son cried a lot, playing his guitar; he died of grief."

I continued to visit him, in search of the rain of fire. I felt it, listening to stories I hadn't heard.

"Do you know Pícol Hill?"

"Yes, *tayta,* you can see it even from Cuzco; also from the road to Paruro; from very far away, you can see that hill."

"They wanted to take that away from us, too. They called out the cavalry guards, but we were prepared."

The guards didn't realize that the road twisted and turned, making it very difficult for them to ascend; they didn't see that the *p'ata kiskas* [cactus] would scratch and threaten them with its spiky bristles; they didn't notice the hatred of the stones, of the pebbles; they didn't understand that if the great red wound in the hill had a human color, that it was from anger, holy anger at seeing guards where there should be only men.

Suddenly some stones moved; they weren't stones, they were Indians, armed with slings like those of the past, like the Indians of time immemorial, with the slings of time immemorial. The slings of the armies of Túpac Amaru, the slings that launched the cry of rebellion: *Warak'as!*[4]

But this time the missiles were not what they had always been, were not Indian stones, but . . . dynamite!

They blocked the head of the column; before they realized what was happening, the horses were on two feet and the guards were on all fours, scurrying down the slope between explosions, disregarding the ferocious spines of the *p'ata kiska,* which are easily detached from the plant, but more difficult to extract from the bodies of people or animals.

"They never returned. It is necessary to fight thus, learn this well, with *warak'a* and with dynamite; with the cunning of the Indians and with the cunning of the mestizos; it is necessary to know well their skills and ours. Keep it up. . . ."

"Yes, *tayta* . . . it is necessary to know well their skills and ours in order to fight better."

And the lessons continued: "Touch my head over here. What do you feel?"

"Soft, *tayta,* there is no bone, indeed, there is only a soft place."

"I am going to tell you about this dent. It was in Oropeza. The Indians were in a lawsuit with the landowner. He had his cronies around, and we were being careful. But on one occasion we had a fiesta and were drinking heavily; then the cronies of the landlord showed up, intent on killing us with clubs."

The ancient antagonists, those of all time, those of the centuries, those of the whole earth: On one side, "the cronies of the landlord"; a mixture of animals and machines, like all those who fight for their masters — be they mercenaries, Yankee marines, Rangers, [5] or traitors. It is an antihuman who wounds human beings. A brutalized machine that doesn't think. To be sure, there is a man inside, but unless brotherhood awakens in him, he remains just that: a machine and a beast, made to hurt human beings.

On the other side, the Indians; symbols of humankind, humanized despite the drunkenness, because now only rebellion converts men into human beings. The Indians, fighting for humanity, for the land; for land for themselves and for all men.

"Suddenly they appeared, yes indeed! One of them grabbed me and broke my head with a club. I fell down for dead, but I revived enough to plunge my knife into him, and then I fell down for dead again. Afterwards — I don't know how much time had passed — I began to hear the ringing of church bells in the distance. 'What's going on?' I said to myself. 'Are they tolling for me or for that *gamonal*'s dog?' After a while, I was able to move a little. I came to and realized that I was alive. Pretty soon I grew calm. 'The bells must have been for the *gamonal*'s crony,' I concluded. So although they may break your head, when you have to go on fighting, you'll come back to life."

"Yes, *tayta.*"

"With judges, the Indians never win; it has to be this way — by fighting. The judges, the guards, all the authorities are on the side of the rich; for the Indian there is no justice. It has to be this way, fighting."

"Yes, *tayta,* just so, fighting."

He told me many more things; he told me that his bones had not been broken when he jumped from a moving train, after they had taken him prisoner.

"Do you tell your professors what I tell you?"

"Only to some, *tayta.*"

"What do they say to you?"

"Some tell me, 'That is so'; they like you, *tayta.* Others tell me, 'Those are foreign ideas.'"

"What is that?"

"I don't know, *tayta.*"

And the lessons in "foreign ideas" continued. Rain of fire. Feeble, cornered, he showered the dying sparks of his life on me. But at times he would explode.

"Damn it! I can no longer fight! These cursed legs will no longer go up the hills. My hands are useless. I am worthless. I can no longer fight! Damn it!"

"Yes, *tayta!* You are going to continue fighting! You are not old, *tayta.* Your feet, your hands are old, to be sure. With my feet you are going with our brothers, *tayta*; with my hands, you are going to fight, *tayta*; it is just as if you were changing your poncho, that's all. My hands, my feet, you are going to use them in order to continue fighting. It is just like changing your poncho, that's all, *tayta!*"

1969

My *Tayta* Jose Maria and the Indian Aspect of the Peruvian Revolution

Arguedas, like Vallejo,[1] is polemical. And it could not be otherwise, considering the many facets of these complex personalities.

Arguedas's personality cannot be resolved into a matter of party membership, literary style, or even his great knowledge of folklore and ethnology. Nevertheless, one would have to be blind — willfully blind, and blind in very bad faith — not to see, or to misconstrue, his very being, his essence. Arguedas, above and before all, is an Indian. He is Indian in the most militant sense of the word.

It is somewhat paradoxical but my *tayta* did not like to use the word *Indian* because it is the whip that the *mestizos* use to beat us, and for that reason among ourselves we say *runa.* He was certainly astonished when I used the term *Indian.*

I tell him, yes, that it is precisely the whip, the whip we have wrenched from the landlord's hands to brandish before his very eyes. For the landlord didn't like it either when we spoke to him in Spanish. And so it has been as Indians, and with our Quechua, that we have raised ourselves up and trampled on them; and in the same way we have used the poncho, the bare feet, and the smell of coca.

The landlords have been brought to their knees trembling, and they will kneel down again. For, although we are opposed to coca and bare feet, we are in that state now, and it is in that state that we are raising ourselves up, and in that state we will crush them.

As the *tayta* José María says, yes, we are liberators for everyone. We, who have been more humble than burros; we, who have been whipped worse than dogs; we, who have been spat upon. Yes, *tayta,* in a word then, we, the *Indians.*

Above all, Arguedas was an Indian. It should be understood that I am not speaking of the percentage of drops in his blood. I speak of his heart, of what he used to call *indio sonqo.*[2]

Contradictions? Of course he had them! But it was the rebellious Indian that set the tone. To conceal that burning truth, some rhetorical juggling is needed.

The simple act of exalting something Indian is already revolutionary. It means showing the world, and the Indian himself, that Indians are people, although they don't want to believe it.

The *huayno,* the *quena,*[3] the Quechua language, the poncho, the legends, the customs; simply by showing them with pride is already to fight, is already to shout the war cry. It shows the Indian himself and it shows everyone that we are a people with a personality and that we have the intention of seeing that that personality is respected.

That is why we revolutionary Indians regard our native tradition with so much respect, with so much fervor. In all its forms, in all its aspects, in all its vigor: Ciro Alegría, Luis E. Valcárcel, José Sabogal, Alviña, J. C. Tello,[4] and so many other beloved names.

Contradictory figures? Yes, doubtless; but all native to this soil, and therefore our forefathers, the revolutionary Indians. Because without them we could never have been. Because we start from the point they reached, from the point to which they led us by the hand.

In the drama *Ollantay*[5] it is not the imperial court that makes an impact. It is the clenched fist of Quechua that jolts us.

And Arguedas is head and shoulders above all of this, as I told my *tayta* in the letter he left half-read. He is no longer only a native; he is the Indian himself, who speaks in his own way, shows his own feelings. He is not Clorinda Matto[6] who takes pity on the Indian's suffering and protests; he is the Indian himself who is rebelling.

And how the *tayta* rebels! With what force! How the passion rises up in the *Yawar Fiesta*,[7] within all Indians to demand that the fiesta be carried out the way they want. Barbarous? Perhaps, but it was done the way the Indians wanted it done, damn it, because the Indians wanted it that way.

And in *Los Rios Profundos*,[8] it is the Indians of the hacienda who, triumphing bare-handed over machine guns, impose their will.

Of course, the well-informed people do not see that this is the whole purpose of that work.

I am not a man of letters, nor am I a literary critic. The literary critics did not see that Arguedas made the great revolutionary potential of the Indian people the central thrust of his work. Only one commented on this subsequently. Distinguished people will tell me that since I am not a literary critic, I should keep my mouth shut and not try to "take over" Arguedas and give his work a forced political interpretation. With all modesty, I have done no more than to repeat literally what was written on the subject by my *tayta* in the week before the bullet.

As he says, he wanted to make the fighters, the political ones, see — so that they would encourage this potential. To be sure, they didn't see! . . . Or they saw too well that it didn't suit them. Because this great revolutionary potential really exists in our people. Because this energy, once freed, tends to look for its own goals and not for compromises and negotiations. Because when the Indian says *manan* [absolutely no], then the *mistis* [non-Indians] know that it's *manan!*[9] Now the distinguished gentlemen are not organizing the *montoneros*, the bands of mountain guerrillas . . . it is not appropriate; that time is past. They know well what the outcome of a *montonero* made up of "them" would be!

Something more: Arguedas does not look for the leader with charisma, even among the Indians themselves. He knows that the strength is not in a leader's power of attraction, in his magnetism, but in the centuries of oppression, and that the leader attracts to the extent that he represents the needs and moods of the people.

The strength is in the Indian's rediscovery of himself, in the Indian's awareness of his potential, in the Indian's development; in his breaking out of the oppressive, anti-Indian, material and mental bondage.

He may begin gropingly, to be sure, as in the novels of Arguedas. But, above all, he is discovering his power! His potential! He brings it to light, he finds it. And that is the beginning.

To whoever may believe that this Indian way of seeing the struggle is chauvinist, regionalist, racist, and opposed to internationalism and even the unity of Peru, we reply that the only way we Indians can become part of humanity is as Indians; it is our way of being people. We have to join the world of peoples as a people, not as a caricature; with a personality, not depersonalized. It is not by accident that the same government that gives the shantytowns the pretty name of "young towns" wants to dissolve us into the general category of "peasants," as if we don't suffer a thousand humiliations precisely because we are Indians.

The Indian problem is the problem of land, as Mariátegui [10] said. It is certainly true, because we know that we have fought, even with guns in our hands, under the slogan "Land or Death!" But our oppression is not simply economic. As a sequel to economic oppression, they abuse the Indians of all our countries in many ways. They destroy our culture, our Quechua, our Aymara, our Guarani, [11] our *yaraví,* [12] our aesthetic values. They spit on us, as the *tayta* says.

The oppression of the Indian people does not have characteristics as marked as the discrimination against Black people in the United States, but it cannot be obliterated by putting the label "peasant" over it.

We understand the unity of our Indian character with our internationalism in the revolutionary way that the universal *cholo* César Vallejo understood it, when he mentions that most

Spanish characteristic of love even to the point of treason; and in the same poem in which he speaks of the universality of the Spanish revolution, he does not contradict those who label it a "Spanish affair"; he agrees and then shows them the sharp internal "Spanish" contradictions of that people in some verses that are models of dialectics.

The Indian struggle is breaking out on all fronts, and that is why we are so grieved by the bullet that shot our *tayta*, for he was a powerful fighter. But if he died in pain, it was with the pain of an Indian who sees the approach of dawn. And, as he said, to suffer with this pain is not to suffer; to die with this pain is not to die.

The Indian struggle, continuing on all fronts, renders a fighter's homáge to José María Arguedas. We who fight directly for the land, like the hacienda Indians and the freeholders of Pasco, Yauyos, Ayacucho, Cuzco, we are not alone. We are accompanied by the *huaynos* of Manuel Acosta Ojeda, of the Pastorita Huaracina, of Jilguero del Huascarán, of "La Sureñita" Lucila Sánchez, [13] and of so many more of our brothers and sisters who fight hard and do not sell out. They do not sell out although they know that the Indian who plays the clown and caricatures his mother and father to make the white man laugh is well paid by his master.

And also fighting at our side are the people who know that the Indian was born when the light had turned to shadow, and who, like Alicia Maguiña, [14] without being Indians themselves, are waiting to hear our laughter in order to be happy.

But the Indian struggle, with all its richness, is only one part of the entire Peruvian revolution. It exists, but there is no reason to exaggerate its importance; it is, I repeat, less than the Afro-American problem in the United States. I speak of it here only because it is the fundamental feature of the *tayta* José María.

The Indian Arguedas understood all this very well; for that reason he was with the university students against the *gorilla* [militarist] law; for that reason he was with the workers' struggles; for that reason he was with Vietnam.

Yes, *tayta* José María, you are right in saying that it will cost much blood, this coming of the dawn, but it is near.

Land or Death! We Will Win!

1969

Peasant Work in the City

One of the principal shortcomings of the peasant movement has been its uneven development. While in some zones it reaches a high level of combativity (although at different times), in others, even though they are adjacent, combativity may be negligible. Another deficiency has been the lack of connection with the struggle of the urban working classes.

It is clear that the fundamental cause is something inherent in the countryside: the vast distances. Unlike the urban proletariat, the peasantry is not concentrated. But countering this drawback, one of the principal features of the peasant movement has been the rapid maturation of its struggle and its rapid rise to higher levels of combativity. The fundamental reason for this is the sharpness of the class contradictions that exist in the countryside. (The agrarian reform law has mitigated these contradictions in part, but it has not destroyed them.)

These features show us that the conscious work of the vanguard must basically aim at extending the peasant movement and not at reinforcing its isolation. In addition, if possible, we must from the outset encourage the liaison of the countryside with the city. Speaking of this, I wrote some time ago: "let us not make a Chaupimayo of each union, let us make a Chaupimayo of Peru."

All this will be achieved through the coordination of the peasant movement. In this coordinating work, the cities, especially Lima, will play the fundamental role.

We must not forget that in Lima centralized organizations already exist in powerful forms, organizations that can bridge the gap between the city and the countryside, organizations composed half of peasants and half of city people.

I refer to the clubs formed according to district and province of origin by Lima residents who are not native to the capital. (The departmental clubs are controlled by the oligarchy.) These people are the key to the Peruvian revolution and to the agrarian revolution in particular. These people who normally live in the slums and shantytowns, who frequent the barbecue stands and amuse themselves in the stadiums. These people who include in their ranks workers, students, and street vendors. And peddlers who crisscross the whole country! Who know the people, the roads, and all sorts of interesting things about Peru. Peddlers, with their packs of merchandise on their backs, who circulate throughout the country like its bloodstream, are the links between Peru's lower classes. All these people who seldom stand out clearly in the urban class struggles, whether they be of the workers or of the students.

These people, underestimated by the "revolutionaries," are very important for us. These people are capable of organizing the countryside and centralizing and coordinating it with the urban movement. Once they have grasped the general ideas, they will apply them better than anyone to the peculiarities of their zones.

The revolutionary city worker has a lot to teach them; but he also has a lot to learn from them and should have enough sense to conduct himself with modesty.

These are the people with whom we are going to work. These are the people we are going to bring to realize how much they are worth, how much they can do, and how much they will do for their land, which they love so much and remember so much, in their *huaynos,* in their football parties, in their cheering at the stadium.

Naturally in the beginning it will only be a tiny minority that will move; the rest will prefer to devote themselves only to social and sports activities. It is always that way, but that is no reason to lose heart. That minority will grow through its own dynamism.

February 1970

Free Vicente Lanado!

Comrade Vicente Lanado was accused of sending food to the guerrillas of the Remigio Huamán Brigade when we were in the mountains. For this crime, he was sentenced *in absentia* to two years in prison by the military tribunal in Tacna.

The comrade was arrested along with other peasants of the zone. They were tortured barbarously. As a result Comrade Carmen Candia died; Vicente Lanado was left with cerebral lesions and impaired vision. The police attacked and completely ransacked his house on various occasions, not even leaving his agricultural tools. They drove off his cattle and other domestic animals. His wife was also imprisoned and tortured. His young children were frightened to such an extent that they still scream with terror when they see a Civil Guard.

After being tortured for ten days, he was sent to prison on December 28, 1962. He was released on bail on April 30, 1963. After the sentence was passed, he was arrested on June 12, 1968. Thus by February 12, 1970, he had completed all told more than the twenty-four months in prison to which he had been sentenced.

It is necessary to take into account that any first offender is paroled after he has completed two-thirds of his sentence. Comrade Vicente Lanado was not only denied this parole, but even now that he has exceeded his two-year term, they refuse to give him his freedom and say that he must be imprisoned for another four months. For that they had no legal pretext.

What happened was that Comrade Vicente Lanado was secretary-general of the Paltaybamba Peasant Union, which he led in an exemplary way. He succeeded in wiping out the feudal-type exploitation that was being carried on by Sebastian Pancorbo and his heirs.

The *gamonales* of this hacienda had had the manor house built at the edge of a very busy road. They set up a "customhouse" and made all who passed stop and pay tribute to the landlord. On one occasion, a Civil Guard was beaten by the landlord for greeting him without removing his cap. The peasants were obliged to climb the steps of the manor house on their knees. The communal villagers of the zone were obliged to work without pay on the hacienda. The landlord stole many coffee plantings from the peasants. He was a member of parliament, a cohort of the president of the Republic, who had made him a present of an alcohol distillery that he had transported "by Indian-back" over many miles of steep and rugged roads. The cultivation of sugar cane for that distillery, and the labor in it, cost the landlord nothing, but the peasants died like flies in that work.

When a peasant died, the landlord would order the family's livestock seized on the pretext that the deceased had owed him money. He had his victims buried in the orchard.

One herdsman fled from his oppression, and the landlord had him captured and ordered him tied hand and foot to four stakes driven into the ground. He whipped him with a lash until he got tired; after resting, he continued whipping until he was exhausted and, after a new rest, again returned to whip-

ping him. Since his hand was aching from the exertion, he
continued the whipping with his hand wrapped in a hand-
kerchief. Afterwards, he had a blacksmith called to shackle
the herdsman's hands to his shoulders with a chain. He became indignant because the chain was slack, and ordered it
tightened with a pliers until the peasant's wrists were bleeding. He left him that way until the following day, when he
had a chain fastened around the herdsman's waist. He then
ordered him to work the fields, watched by an employee who
held him by a rope tied to the chain belt. At night the herdsman was locked up with his family, and in the morning he
was obliged to work at the end of the rope.

It would take a long time to tell all the atrocities of this distinguished gentleman, national deputy and then senator. His
heirs follow in his footsteps.

These things do not constitute crimes in Peru; to oppose
them, however, does constitute an unpardonable crime; to abol-
ish this state of affairs is an even greater crime. That is why
they don't release Vicente Lanado; in spite of his having served
more than his sentence.

For the union led by Vicente Lanado, an illiterate peasant
who speaks only Quechua, swept away this exploitation, built
schools, used social labor for social benefit, and redeemed
human dignity for the peasantry of the area, after driving
out the *gamonal.*

The exploiters' government repressed the union violently,
installed a post of the Civil Guard in the manor house, and
jailed the union leaders. Vicente Lanado paid with sixteen
months in prison for this "crime," in addition to the two years
he is serving for sending food to us in the mountains.

Comrade Vicente Lanado, from prison, publicly protested
the massacre of peasants of Huanta and Ayacucho. The un-
yielding defense of his class brothers on the part of this self-
sacrificing, unlettered peasant is the true cause of the bitter-
ness of the exploiters' government against him.

The eight small children of the peasant Vicente Lanado are
homeless; they do not even have the bread of their own poverty to eat. The government has exposed itself by its treatment
of this peasant and his children.

This is the same government that says: Peasant, the landlord will no longer grow fat on your poverty.

February 1970

The Earthquake: The Rich and the Poor

Each day we hear on the radio and read in the bourgeois newspapers, both official and privately owned, that the earthquake,[1] like any other natural catastrophe, makes no class distinctions. We hear and read the daily sermon that in times like these we must forget all class differences.

One part of my education as a revolutionary was to be injured in an earthquake (Cuzco, 1950). For this reason, and as a militant of the FIR, it is my duty to speak on the subject — especially in view of the fact that this will not be the last time Peruvian revolutionaries will be confronted with such a situation. Since we live in a country abounding in natural catastrophes, it is appropriate to discuss the subject.

Before speaking of the consequences, let us not forget that the geographer Edmundo Roy and many other Peruvian scientists have pointed to the French atomic explosion opposite the disaster zone on the preceding day as either the direct or possible cause of the earthquake (which snuffed out at least fifty thousand lives, and left a million direct casualties, about a tenth of the country's population). The official agencies, of course, have rejected this opinion, affirming that it is an accidental coincidence — like the other natural tragedies that followed immediately on the heels of previous French explosions.

This tragedy is being exploited by the bourgeois politicians and corporations to develop a campaign of widespread demogogy about their philanthropy, giving as "relief" a tiny part of the huge sums they amass from the sweat of the workers. Many firms, known for their inhumanity to their workers, are trying to present a humanitarian facade that will permit them more easily to exploit the workers they employ, and thus to regain with interest their "relief" contribution.

The case of the Cerro de Pasco Copper Corporation is instructive. While it waxes eloquent about its aid in rebuilding one of the highways, it raised obstacles to the donation of one day's salary, which the workers wanted to give and which the trade union had called for; the union was obliged to use a strike threat to force the company's compliance.

It also fits in that the U. S. government should try to appear humanitarian, showing us, among other things, that its helicopters are used to save lives (the same helicopters used in its genocide in Indochina, and which will probably return to Peru on another occasion to save the life of the capitalist system and of U. S. imperialist domination). Not even the

Peruvian repressive forces are missing the chance to gain prestige and to help the people whom they readily massacre when those same people struggle against their exploiters. France sends us geologists.

In addition, this tragedy is being utilized to the utmost by the exploiters to try to convince us that we are all one people, and that we must put aside rancor. The "left-wing" servants of the junta are the first to insist that strikes should now be called off.

But counterposed to the hypocrisy of those who thrive precisely on the misery of the people is the authentic solidarity of the workers, students, and all the exploited sectors of the country, as well as our brothers in other countries.

Many unions have democratically voted to donate a day's wages for the injured.

The students of medicine, social work, the Agricultural School, among others, have rushed to the disaster zone, putting their knowledge and efforts at the service of their suffering people.

The secondary-school students have mobilized to take collections.

The market workers have contributed food, as they did previously for the striking workers.

The poor from all sectors have taken the bread out of their own hungry mouths to send to their brothers in the north. They have given up their own miserable winter clothing to alleviate, at the cost of their own shivering, that of their injured brothers. They have donated part of the meager blood left them by the exploiters for the benefit of the injured. This is the solidarity of the poor — from Cuba, Chile, and other countries as well.

We must not forget the nurses, the soldiers, and all those who, although they are part of the state apparatus, put their love for their people into incessant work, without taking time out to sleep. We must not confuse them with the glutted, greedy, hypocritical bureaucracy. They are the opposite poles of the same institutions. Like the peasants and the workers, they are the exploited not the exploiters.

The popular mobilization during this tragedy is very important. One clear manifestation was the spontaneous, immediate, and indignant rejection by the people of the irresponsible efforts to celebrate a football victory in the streets at a time of popular grief. The alienation systematically produced by the creators of "public opinion" had not succeeded in numbing the sensibilities of our people.

The solidarity of the workers is a positive force in their struggles against natural catastrophes and exploiters; it is an indispensable element of the revolution. For this reason, although we reject the opportunist position that now we are all one people, which is a suitable position for class collaborationists, we do not make the sectarian mistake of refusing to participate in and build the authentic popular mobilization on the pretext that it plays into the hands of the diversionists or that it is "philanthropy." We participate in and build the mobilization with our own class position.

The poor are affected most. The idea that "the earthquake does not discriminate" is a lie. The adobe huts of the poor have crumbled to dust; the cement houses of the rich are still standing.

But the earthquake's real discrimination takes place not at the very moment of the quake, but afterwards. Immediately the prices of food, clothing, blankets, materials that can serve for tents, and medicines rise exorbitantly. Only the wealthy can afford them. The poor are condemned to die of hunger, cold, and neglected injuries. The majority of the deaths come after the earthquake, although official statistics do not recognize them as its victims.

During quakes like those in Cuzco or in Ancash, which occurred in the dead of winter at more than 3,000 meters [9,842.5 feet] above sea level, the cold that freezes water kills many people who must sleep in the open or only half-sheltered, especially the children, the elderly, and the sick. This cold kills more easily than at any other time because the people are hungrier than normal, without calories to protect them.

For the rich, there is an abrupt decline in their luxury, opulence, and comfort. For the poor, there is an abrupt decline in their chances of survival.

The authorities and the daily papers give us horrified accounts of "human vultures." So they describe the looters, and they tell us that they have given orders to shoot them.

Who are these looters? At first, they are generally habitual petty thieves who benefit from these situations of confusion as from others. But then, as the days pass, the looters are poor people who literally have neither bread nor grain to eat and who want to survive. They are more likely to get a bullet than bread. And so the character of the bourgeois state is dramatically displayed. For this purpose, one of the first measures of the government is to send forces of law and order, to impose a curfew. So that the poor will starve to death in an orderly and disciplined fashion.

The real vultures are the official functionaries charged with collecting and distributing assistance. Anyone who has ever been the victim of an earthquake or similar disaster will remember being the victim of these vultures.

In Cuzco, the volunteer census-takers (students), who were sent by the bureaucrats, were at first viewed with affection and hope by the injured; gradually we became hated, and were finally nearly stoned because the bureaucrats sent out brigade after brigade to take the census, to investigate how many there were and what they needed, but never distributed the relief. To be sure, they distributed some of it afterwards (afterwards! when many had already died for lack of it), but that was only a small part of all the aid that came from the rest of the country and from abroad, and which was given such wide publicity by the daily papers and radio stations. We even saw much of that aid arrive at the prefecture, but we never saw it leave. (A very popular saying was that the only tower that benefited from the earthquake was Torreblanca, the prefect.) [2]

We also knew that the aid sent during the Cuzco drought was so scandalously plundered that they felt obliged to start an investigation. Nevertheless, when the judge (Dr. Valer) ordered the appearance in court of the two ex-ministers who were implicated in the plundering, they immediately changed judges. (A few years later they imprisoned Dr. Valer as an "extremist" in La Sepa Penal Camp, deep in the jungle, as a consequence of which he died.)

Renrahirca [3] protested for years because the celebrated relief never arrived.

In none of the tragedies has there been any lack of these vultures of the bureaucracy, vultures who have caused the death of untold numbers of our brothers and sisters. Against these vultures there is no order to shoot.

The aid that succeeds in reaching the disaster zone is distributed in accordance with the economic and social level of the victims. This is not to say that they give the most to the poorest people; on the contrary, they give little or nothing to the poorest people. The influential people receive the best and the most relief. (In the *Plaza de Armas* in Cuzco, after the earthquake, the family of a *commandante* was installed in immense tents, one of which was their reception room, while poor families didn't have even a blanket for shelter.)

How can these problems be solved immediately? We must

solve these problems from two angles: the relief sector and the injured sector.

We must fight to see that that the relief from the popular sectors is as organized, direct, and centralized as possible. It is very good that the unions, the associations in the slums, and the university federations are acting organizationally to collect aid and to collaborate in their own work in the affected zones. We must make sure that the secondary-school students also organize democratically to offer their help.

We agree that the CGTP [General Confederation of Peruvian Workers] should coordinate this assistance, but they must do it in a democratic way, through representatives elected by the rank and file, and with strict control by that rank and file. Aid must be distributed by commissions sent by the workers and the students themselves.

The more we do without the corrupt state bureaucracy, which has not been elected by the people and is not controlled by them, the better. Centralization, coordination, and planning, yes; but by the people's organizations, and democratically.

We must give impetus to the organization of earthquake victims in committees or associations designed to look after their immediate and future interests. They should, of course, not only participate as directly as possible in controlling distribution of the immediate relief, but they should also be alert to all questions relative to their collective future: reconstruction, orphans, and so forth.

The provincial and district associations, and those of the Lima residents, have a very important role to play in this work. As for the Ancash Club (departmental),[4] we know that it is a den of *gamonales* and their cohorts.

Immediate relief is indispensable, but it does not completely solve the problem of injured people. We must demand more far-reaching emergency measures:

● Immediate agrarian reform, distribution of the land to the peasants with no compensation.

● Nationalization under workers' control of the industrial centers of the zone, channeling profits into the reconstruction of the region, again under workers' control.

It is monstrous that this government, which calls itself revolutionary and puts on a big show of making supreme efforts to help the earthquake victims, should try to collect a single cent from the peasants, to whom it would be more appropriate to distribute the lands. Or that it should permit the efforts of the injured workers to go toward satisfying the greed of the capitalists.

● A special tax on the profits of the capitalists throughout the country (whether native- or foreign-owned enterprises), to be spent on reconstruction of the affected zone.

● Reconstruction of towns in locations that are not dangerous. It must be taken into account that relatively safe sites exist, but they are off limits for building towns because they have private owners. That was the case with the town of Santa María in La Convención. Many lives were lost between the hill and the river while there was a safe site opposite whose owner was a *gamonal.* The desperate population of Santa María asked for the help of our peasant organization and, under its protection, occupied the area to rebuild their town. For several months we have seen shantytowns built in Lima on the banks of the Rímac River, slums that have been swept away by floods while the burghers of San Isidro and Orrantia putter happily on their enormous golf courses, or enjoy life in immense mansions in the middle of stretches of green countryside.

We propose these transitional measures, keeping in mind that we are acting within a capitalist society. But we know that the final solution that our people must employ to confront natural tragedies such as this is the socialist organization of the country.

A socialist Peru will organize the entire national resources from top to bottom, without need of bourgeois philanthropy. There will be no need to beg individual owners, the businessmen, to lend means of transportation, the lack of which is costing many lives. The graduates of the Agricultural School will not have to go begging for the tools to open up roads which will bring help. The people will do all that in an organized fashion, without having to beg anything of anyone. The Cuban harvests and the accomplishments of the Cuban people after Hurricane Flora have shown us what this power means.

In a socialist Peru, there will be no problem of mass unemployment, nor of the injured and disabled, nor will there be an orphan problem: in a socialist Peru no child will be an orphan.

June 1970

The Government, the Oligarchy, and the Exploited

There is confusion among the left about this government, whether or not it is anti-oligarichical. The obscurity of the term "oligarchy" contributes to this confusion. If in our country we understand the word "oligarchy" to refer to the cotton- and sugar-producing sectors, and the system of *gamonalismo* common to the sierra, we can indeed say that this government is anti-oligarchical. But if by "oligarchy" we mean government by a wealthy and powerful group, we cannot certify the junta as anti-oligarchical: we must say that it represents more the new oligarchy which is displacing the old; or more accurately, it is in large measure absorbing and incorporating the old oligarchy into itself, voluntarily or by force.

Our country has been and is a semicolony of imperialism, fundamentally Yankee imperialism. Imperialism in its classical form was characterized by its retardation of capitalist development in the backward countries, which were kept as sources of raw materials and importers of manufactured articles. Our countries were plantations and mines complementary to the manufacturing countries in the imperialist economy. Within this context, the principal allies of imperialism in our country were the cotton and sugar magnates, the *gamonales* of the sierra, the importers and exporters, and the banks, which were linked to all those sectors. We might characterize them as groups interested in maintaining the backwardness of our country.

The industrial and manufacturing bourgeoisie, interested in the capitalist development of the country, was weak. Nonetheless, the industrial sector was gathering strength little by little, primarily because some imperialist companies began to realize that it was cheaper and more convenient to build factories in our country, near the sources of raw materials, paying the cheap *cholo* labor in Peruvian currency, and manufacturing products in the country where they were going to be sold (instead of transporting the raw materials to their country, paying the relatively high wages of the North American workers, and then sending the finished products back to be sold in Peru). Even some industries that had to import raw materials chose this alternative, and even assembly plants avoided the import duty on finished products by importing the component parts of automobiles and other manufactured items.

Furthermore, the families of the old oligarchy broadened their activities, directing them toward the industrial sector, some more, others less. Names like Aspíllaga, Pardo, Prado, and De la Piedra began to appear in the manufacturing industries.

The growth of industry in our country and in the imperialist countries required more consumers. The peasant masses, who were largely self-sufficient, represented a promising potential market. However, although they were slowly becoming purchasers of industrial products, there was a great barrier that seriously obstructed any acceleration of this process: the old agrarian structure, the semifeudal relations of production, in which the peasant did not get wages for his work, but only the right to cultivate a small plot of land for his subsistence. [1] For this reason, the national and imperialist industrial sectors regarded agrarian reform as necessary for themselves.

In addition, we should take into account that the imperialist sectors that produce machinery had an increasing interest in the industrial development of our country, which would absorb their products, even though this industrialization was to be accomplished by the state and the national capitalists.

The colonial revolutions that remained within the framework of capitalism taught the imperialists that agrarian reform and industrialization, no matter how "nationalist" they might be, if they did not go beyond capitalism, would stimulate the imperialist economy, not only by the import of new consumers' goods, but also by the import of machinery.

There exist, therefore, important sectors of imperialism that are interested in the industrial capitalist development of our country.

With the progress of industrialization, the demand increased for engineers and technicans that were being turned out by the national and foreign universities. However, since their number exceeds the requirements of the present industrialization, they, along with other sectors of the middle class that are linked to industrial production, are a new element clamoring for further economic development.

The above-mentioned sectors are those particularly interested in the capitalist industrial development of the country. We have underscored the role of the imperialist sectors because that is the aspect that the opportunists do not see, or do not want to see: an adapted aspect of imperialism in this epoch of neocapitalism which differentiates it from its former characteristic opposition to the industrial development of our countries.

In addition to the individual interests of these sectors in the capitalist industrial development of the country, there is the general interest of all the exploitative sectors, native as well as imperialist, in saving the capitalist system; and the only way of saving it is through industrial development. Therefore, the most enlightened among the exploitative sectors in general are in favor of the capitalist industrial development of the country. (There are those who attribute importance only to this factor, but we disagree with that opinion.)

If the forces interested in the removal of the old oligarchy have become so powerful and can also count on popular support for that removal, then why was the repression necessary? Precisely because of the great danger that that mobilization of popular support represents for the exploiters.

The parlimentary system was not suitable for carrying out the change. When the contending interests among all the exploitative sectors showed themselves "democratically" — not only the old oligarchy versus the pro-development sectors, but even the differences among the latter, with each one now fighting for his own interests — when they carried on an open discussion, they found that they had stimulated the participation of the people as a whole in the discussion. The no-holds-barred popular debate that ensued was seriously undermining the authority of the governing classes.

APRA, shamefaced over its revolutionary past, had to conduct itself in a completely servile manner before the old oligarchy (represented fundamentally in that parliamentary period by the UNO)[2] whose favor it was currying.

The AP-DC "Alliance"[3] could have overwhelmed the reactionary sectors by appealing to the popular masses. But what all exploiters fear most is precisely the mobilization of the masses. Confident of that timidity and vacillation on the part of the representatives of the pro-development sectors, the old oligarchy, and the imperialist sectors linked to it, prevailed. Not only did they render the agrarian reform law inoperable, but they ultimately forced the government to capitulate shamefully with respect to the nationalization of the rich oil deposits in La Brea and Pariñas.

The "page eleven scandal,"[4] on top of the uselessness of the agrarian reform law, clearly demonstrated Belaúnde's failure in his reformist intentions, and this was dangerous not only because these were two measures necessary for development, but because they were two problems about which the people had acquired great awareness. But this was not only the failure of Belaúndism: it also showed the impossibility of carrying out bourgeois reforms in a parliamentary regime without a "dangerous" mobilization of the masses.

Therefore, the coup was necessary for the pro-development sectors to carry out in a planned way the measures urgently required to encourage economic development and save the system.

As many have indicated, the armed forces in many countries have been converted into the bourgeois political party par excellence, the party that has come to supersede the completely discredited politicians. This of course does not mean that the same frictions and antagonisms do not exist within the armed forces as within the exploitative sectors, whom they represent. Nevertheless, the military organism has the advantage that the antagonisms in it are kept secret, internal, are not debated openly, and do not agitate the people.

We characterize the present regime as Bonapartist because it represents all the exploitative sectors as a whole, and its basic objective is to save the save the system. Nevertheless, its plan for saving the system favors the bourgeois pro-development sectors more than any others, and it identifies more with their special interests.

The greatest friction within the government is with the old oligarchy and the classic imperialist interests. The present regime has taken important measures, greatly affecting those sectors, for the benefit of the industrialized sector: The agrarian reform law, despite all its limitations, tends to destroy the latifundias, spur production, and create layers of a peasant petty bourgeoisie with a purchasing power allowing them to be incorporated into the capitalist market. In addition, the form of expropriation (with industrial vouchers) forces the *gamonales* to become capitalists in manufacturing industry. They remain exploiters, but they are forced to change the form of exploitation.

The strengthening of the bourgeois state within the national economy is characteristic of neocapitalism, as much in backward countries as in the advanced countries. Impelled by the danger of the collapse of the capitalist system if it continues at the mercy of the struggle for greater profits by the national exploiters, they themselves have come to realize that they need an increasingly strong bourgeois state, one with greater decision-making power within the economic process, that can steer effectively enough to save capitalism from shipwreck.

That is the reason for the famous "plan." That is why the state tends to take charge of the public utilities (energy sources, communications, transportation, etc.), basic industry, and other levers of the economy. For that reason, the junta has nationalized the refining and marketing of copper and other minerals, has nationalized the marketing of fishmeal, has strengthened the state bank, controls currency exchange, is nationalizing telephone service, strengthening the Gas Company of Peru, and so forth.

It is attempting to take into its hands the levers of the economy so that the economy will develop as smoothly as possible for the benefit of the capitalists, with the object of properly providing the factories with everything they need for easy maintenance of maximum profits. And that is economic development — of the capitalist economy, of course.

The educational reform is nothing more than a complement of these measures. The Peruvian educational system was an anachronism. The product of a feudal society, designed for the aristocracy; it has merely undergone some patchwork on its upper levels, though it is certain that on these levels student intervention had considerably modified the administrative system of the universities. In contrast, the primary and secondary levels were practically untouched. The massive popular influx into those grades, which had been designed for a select minority that was supposed to go on to higher studies, threw the whole educational system into chaos.

Now the government has reformed the elementary and grammar school levels so that they will supply the personnel for an industrial society, that is, skilled labor. This is undoubtedly an advance. However, the imposition of this requirement on the universities has meant a retreat, rescinding in practice student co-government, which, among other things, had expressed the struggle for a university at the service of the people, and not at the service of the exploiters, either old or new, imperialist or native, *gamonales* or capitalists.

The government also has conflicts with the industrial sectors, and proof of this is the discord regarding the industrial law. This discord has served to show more clearly than ever the Bonapartist character of the regime: for while the National Society of Industries is looking out for the immediate interests of the capitalists with the myopic ambition characteristic of individual exploiters, the junta, as the general representative of all the exploiters, takes care of the historic interests of the industrial bourgeoisie.

The efforts to become less dependent on imperialism are another proof of the Bonapartist character of the government; but this does not mean that it is anti-imperialist, since, as we have seen, the bourgeois development of the country is taking place in the context of the general interests of imperialism in the epoch of neocapitalism.

The Left

A great part of the left has capitulated contemptibly before this bourgeois government. In the front ranks is the pro-Moscow Communist Party, delighted at seeing confirmed in reality the Stalinist theory of the progressive bourgeoisie. At its side are the old-type opportunists, for instance, the FLN,[5] and individual "personalities." Even pseudo-Trotskyists such as the Pabloite Frías and the Posadistas of *Voz Obrera* (Workers Voice) have joined hands beneath the junta's banner of "revolution," discovering that "reality takes precedence over theory," and undergoing self-criticism for their old positions.

All these groups capered with joy when they received Fidel's blessing for their capitulation. All together and in various posts, they are playing a relatively important role as servants of the government, to disorient and housebreak the mass movement.

Other groups on the left maintain their sectarian positions without having noted in practice any change of importance in the real situation in Peru. Some of them even characterize the present regime as fascist, and draw no distinction between it and the ultraright. They isolate themselves from the masses, who have certain illusions about this government and have not yet learned from this experience. Those comrades make no serious effort to work with the masses in their immediate struggles. This ultraleft position has been bolstered because the regime's most reactionary actions have been directed against the university, the environment of these groups.

The Trotskyist FIR, the Peruvian section of the Fourth International, maintains the position that Marxists have always upheld in similar cases. We support the progressive measures of this government, but we do not support the bourgeois government's defense of the capitalist system through reforms.

The FIR takes into account the present state of the class struggle thoughout the country and on each front, and sets out from reality to raise the level of popular struggles, guiding them toward the capture of power through the inevitable step of the violent destruction of the bourgeois state at the hands of the working masses organized for combat.

We have no illusions about the gradual transformation of the exploiters' state into a socialist state, regardless of how reformist the bourgeois government shows itself to be. Neither do we have illusions about the miraculous effects of desperate actions, heroic and spectacular though they may be, when they have nothing to do with the actual process of the masses learning through their own struggle; within that struggle, indeed, heroic acts are fruitful and inspiring and can serve as detonators of greater explosions.

The FIR learns more and more how to rise above the opportunist prostration or adventuristic desperation, which are often intermixed and connected, as we see in so many current examples.

The Government and the Masses

The junta is making maximum use of all the reformist measures for a great campaign of demagogic propaganda. It presents itself as anti-imperialist, as the executor of a unique historical process, neither capitalist nor socialist, but "Peruvian." It presents itself as the redeemer of the peasantry, continuator of the fight of Túpac Amaru, nationalist to the marrow, indisputably revolutionary.

For this campaign, it counts on a battalion of "leftists" and opportunists of every variety. Even the ultraright lends credence to this demogogy so that it can attack the junta from its own stone-age positions. Nevertheless, the junta's fear of progovernment mass mobilizations is notorious. The support meeting of the slums and the support meeting of the CGTP terrified the junta. It has seen the inability of the servile bureaucrats to confine these mobilizations within the desired limits. The much-touted Committees for the Defense of the Revolution are only ridiculous groups of opportunists, careerists, and bureaucrats. Although this is due in part to the lack of enthusiasm among the masses, who could give them real life, it is also due to the government's fear of any type of popular mobilization.

The fundamental problems confronting the working class continue to be the rising cost of living and unemployment.

The CTP [Confederation of Peruvian Workers], led by APRA, which had already been widely discredited before the coup, remained almost totally deflated afterwards. It can no longer deceive the workers with talk about support by the APRA legislators and functionaries, who have been tossed overboard.

The CGTP, led by the pro-Moscow Communist Party, is becoming stronger despite its bureaucratism and opportunism. The workers, although they have not given their confidence to the government, have certain hopes of success in stemming the offensive of the bosses by means of the CGTP's support of the government. The CGTP goes around proclaiming that "the ministry of labor still has not put itself in tune with the revolution," instead of showing that the ministry's anti-working-class positions prove precisely that it is very much in tune with the bourgeois pro-development reformists.

The support-the-government meeting convoked by the CGTP was very significant, not only because it showed the servility of the Communist Party bureaucrats, but also because it became clear that the unions were using the meeting to raise their own demands. The posters and language of the unions were at bottom characterized by working-class demands, and support to the government was displayed with the hope that through that support their demands would be heard.

The proletariat is waging a continuous daily struggle, often militant and heroic, in defense of its rights. Unfortunately, this struggle suffers from extreme decentralization. The support of the CGTP to the struggling unions is purely verbal.

Unfortunately, for decades the working class in Peru has had no tradition of coordinated struggle for its demands. For this reason, among others, it still does not exert pressure on the CGTP bureaucracy, demanding nationwide battles; and in general it demands of the CGTP only more effective support to isolated conflicts.

Our immediate task within the working-class movement is oriented to the democratic organization of the struggles, organization that leads in the direction of their coordination and centralization, and to the methodical use of the mass mobilization on various levels as the fundamental weapon. This is the aim of our fight for support to unions that are engaged in struggles, for their coordination, for the presentation of a unified set of demands by region and by industrial branch, advancing to the struggle for a nationally unified set of demands.

Part of this struggle is our continual effort to strengthen and democratize the unions, the regional federations, the federations of industry, and the CGTP itself. The Trotskyists, taking into account the present stage of the class struggle, see this work within the workers' movement as the best means of raising its consciousness, its organization, and its struggle to higher levels. There are broad layers of vanguard unionists who concur with us on these immediate trade-union demands. It is our duty to organize this entire vanguard, on all levels, around a common trade-union program. Only in that way will we acquire enough forces in our struggle against the bosses and their government, and against the opportunist and treacherous bureaucracy.

The peasants continue to suffer from the lack of an organization that will organize them on a national scale. Although they have more reason than the working class to support the government, they are less ingenuous than they seem. The repression directed against them by former regimes and even this one, through use of the armed forces, lingers on in their memory and keeps them suspicious, although it also hinders their mobilization. The manipulations of the state bureaucracy in applying the agrarian reform law reinforce that suspicion. However, it is not possible to draw many generalizations with respect to the peasantry, for their political level is more varied, according to region and according to social layer, than is the case with the working class.

The opportunists are trying to orient the peasants toward total support for the government and toward following behind the agrarian reform law. The sectarians, having rejected the law, isolate themselves from the peasants, thus doing the government and the opportunists a big favor.

We must elaborate a transitional program that will make use of all the positive aspects of the law in order to stimulate the peasant movement and its democratic control of the cooperatives and of the entire process of agrarian reform, as well as the defense of the peasant organizations. Orienting ourselves fundamentally to the lowest layers, we must continue to make concerted efforts towards organizing and centralizing the peasant movement.

Within these general outlines, our work will have many variations in each specific case, for example:

● La Convención (Cuzco) — Not one cent in payment for the lands that we have conquered in our struggle and that are already in our hands. Organization of the agricultural laborers, who will be a powerful support for the militant vanguard that is at the forefront of the provincial federation and that has to fight the negative pressure of the rich peasants. Publicity about the victories in Chaupimayo where the peasants have kept farms they seized and work them collectively for the benefit of the community as a whole, after having rejected all government attempts to make them pay for those farms, farms which they created with their own sweat and tears and conquered by their own strength.

● Cooperatively owned industrial haciendas — fight for total control of these enterprises by the democratically organized workers. Democratic reorganization and defense of the unions.

● Communal villages whose lands were stolen by the *gamonales* — return of lands belonging to the villages, without compensation, and their distribution as decided democratically by the peasants. Annulment of the expropriation if there was any.

● Haciendas that have been declared partially or totally exempt — inspection of their exemption status by democratically elected representatives of the peasants.

The students constitute the popular sector that is most antigovernment, among other reasons because it has been the most oppressed by the present regime. The university law stamped out student co-government in order to put the university totally at the service of the bourgeoisie. Of the 18,000 applicants to San Marcos, the country's principal university, only 2,500 were admitted.

However, this sector, which in general has a revolutionary socialist consciousness, has been characterized by self-imposed confinement within the university, by the sectarianism, bureaucracy, and adventurism which still afflict it. The students tend to have their heads in the clouds. Ultraleft ideology predominates in their milieu and produces much talk about socialism and armed struggle, but owing to the lack of a transitional program based on actual conditions, the struggle boils down in practice to sporadic and desperate spontaneous actions that follow no plan of struggle, actions weakened by sectarian divisions and isolation from the rest of the population.

To overcome this state of affairs, it is necessary to fight for the revitalization of the student organizations through a thorough and democratic discussion with full participation of the rank and file on how to struggle against the university law and for the general demands of the Peruvian people. The plan of action must include not only propaganda in all sectors of the population about the significance of the undemocratic university law, but also the fusion of the consciously revolutionary student elements with the masses of workers and peasants, thus stimulating the present struggles of the workers of the countryside and of the city, while always taking into account their degree of consciousness and the relationship of forces.

This means taking care not to become separated from the masses by flying into the clouds, avoiding taking positions that do not correspond to the present level of consciousness of the masses of workers and peasants and that would be readily taken advantage of by the reaction, the government, and the opportunists, to discredit the students in the eyes of the workers and thus isolate them. Fortunately, there are indications that this fusion is beginning to occur.

The Need For a Party

All the work that the vanguard elements carry out within the students', workers', and peasants' movements, and on other fronts (in the slums and the forgotten villages, for instance) around general democratic demands will be diluted, will lose its force, and will have no perspective for a serious advance unless they are coordinated by a consciously revolutionary organization that can group together the best elements of that vanguard, serving them by providing the lessons of the class struggle all over the world, current as well as past; by a mutual exchange of experiences, analyzing them, discussing them; by enriching their strategy in this way, defining the place of their own struggle within that of the entire Peruvian people, and combining the struggle on various fronts in a conscious manner.

Whoever denies the need for workers, peasants, or students to organize in unions or federations can be classified as a sellout; and with good reason, since the principle that unity makes strength, the principle in which we must organize and discipline ourselves in order to fight, is so evident that only sellouts would reject it. Equally reactionary results come from denying, even in good faith, the need for vanguard elements from the various fronts of the struggle to form an organization — democratic, centralized and consciously revolutionary.

The FIR has begun the building of that party formed by revolutionary fighters on all fronts. We respect the struggle of those elements that have no party; we consider that their struggle serves the advance of the Peruvian revolution, but we know that their effect would be many times greater if they formed an organization. Therefore, we issue an urgent call to all those comrades to help us build the party that will organize and lead the struggle of the workers, starting from present conditions, to the very destruction of the bourgeois state and the construction of socialism with the workers in power.

July 1970

To the Peasants of La Convencion and Lares*

El Frontón Penal Colony
July 1970

Comrades:

I have been invited by the leaders of our federation to speak at this meeting. I cannot attend personally, but I am at your side in the struggle; and I will always be there, until they kill me.

In these moments, when many people believe that the exploiters are making gifts of the land to the peasants because they have had a change of heart, we must make Peru remember the history of La Convención and Lares. Here we have won the land through our organization and our struggle.

The governments and the authorities were always in the service of the *gamonales;* many laws were passed in our behalf, but they never gave us justice through their legal channels.

It was not enough for the peasants to organize in unions and federations. We had to show our strength and determination to struggle — through meetings, work stoppages, strikes, and similar actions. Finally, we had to form a peasant guerrilla band, the Remigio Huamán Union Brigade, to make them respect our rights. We were few in number in the guerrilla band, but its example made the exploiters see that if they tried to return the land to the *gamonales,* the entire peasantry would rise up in arms. Therefore, the land remains in our hands. Now they want us to pay for that land, as if the work and blood of so many years is not worth a thousand times more than the land they stole.

To pay for our land, which has been regained by our own efforts, would mean to betray heroes such as Simón Oviedo and Benito Cutipa, would mean to betray those of us who are prisoners. This land we have won with our organization and our struggle, and with this organization and this struggle we will defend it. For this reason we repeat our cry "Land or Death!"

The system of *gamonalismo* and all the exploiters are in

---

* This message was read aloud to the July 26, 1970, rally in Cuzco called by the Provincial Peasants Federation of the Valleys of La Convencion and Lares [H. B.].

great fear of our unions and our federations, and they know that while those unions and federations exist, they will not be able to smash the peasantry. Therefore, they wage war against the unions and the federation in every way. And therefore, the government does not want to recognize the federation, or turn the cooperatives over to the unions and the federations, which are the authentic representatives of the peasantry. They have always tried to destroy our organization, sometimes with massacres and jailings, and other times with bribes and sweet words. They promise miracles to get the peasants to desert their organizations.

Some people have allowed themselves to be deceived, especially wealthy ex-tenant farmers. The scheme of the exploiters is to ally with them to crush the poor peasants and the agricultural laborers, and they think that after crushing us it will be easy for them to show the door to the wealthy ex-tenant farmers, whom they have deluded.

Those comrades must understand that if they help smash the peasants and their federation, the government's sweet reasonableness toward them will not last very long, for the exploiters will seize their land and there will be no one to defend them. Perhaps we do not remember that there has never been justice for the peasants? Perhaps we have forgotten that only with our strength, through our struggle, will we succeed in getting justice.

There are other comrades who do not want to let the agricultural laborers into the unions and the federation. Those comrades should understand that the agricultural laborers will be the decisive force for our organization, the agricultural laborer comrades will never be deceived, and will never have illusions like those of the rich peasants who are going over to the side of the enemy. Long live the agricultural laborer comrades!

Finally comrades, we must understand that the struggle has not ended with the recovery of our land; that it will not end until the land of the whole country, and the factories and mines, are in the hands of the Peruvian workers. The struggle will not end until the toilers install a workers' and peasants' government. I do not speak of a government that claims to be on the side of the peasants, nor a government that emerges from the elections that the capitalists hold. I speak of a government composed of delegates of the organizations of the toilers. A government formed by the delegates of our federation, elected by the rank and file, together with comrades elected from all the rank-and-file formations in Peru.

As long as we do not have that, the struggle will continue, regardless of our wishes. The exploiters are only hoping that our unions and our federation will grow weaker, so that they can take back all the conquests of the peasants of La Convención. We already know that when they are strong, they sweep away laws and property titles in an instant; to them those laws are just garbage.

Therefore, the peasants of La Convención and Lares must pay attention to the struggle of the workers, the peasants, and the students of the whole country, as well as to the other sections of the population. Ours is one struggle, and to raise and advance it we must strengthen our organizations, we must support the struggles of all the workers and students. Finally, we must coordinate our struggle so that battles are waged in unison, so that the government cannot weaken us by fighting us separately, sector by sector.

Our struggle has begun successfully as a struggle for the land with our slogan of "Land or Death!" But it cannot end there. Our struggle will continue until all the land of Peru is in the hands of the peasants; until the factories and the mines are in the hands of the workers; until education is for everyone; until we have a workers' and peasants' government; until the exploitation of man by man is wiped out; until the triumph of socialism.

For all of this, our glorious cry of "Land or Death!" which is still valid and militant, must be accompanied on this twenty-sixth of July by the cry raised by our Cuban brothers, in the first socialist republic of America, in whose footsteps we follow: *Patria o Muerte! Venceremos!*

Hugo Blanco G.

Notes

Chapter 1

1. *General Odría.* Former military dictator of Peru. Led 1945 coup which overthrew the APRA-backed president and the APRA-dominated congress; held presidency from 1948 to 1956 when he acquiesced to elections and was succeeded by Prado.

2. *Michel Pablo.* A former leader of the Fourth International; the foremost advocate in the 1950s of the strategy of abandoning attempts to build independent Trotskyist parties in favor of entering the mass Stalinist and social-democratic parties; the rationale was the imminence of World War III and the belief that under conditions of war and international class struggle, revolutionary wings would develop in those parties; he also viewed the degenerated and deformed workers' states as an inevitable and long-term stage of postcapitalist development. Pablo's policies provoked a split in the world Trotskyist movement which was healed only at the Fourth International's reunification congress in 1963; shortly thereafter Pablo split from the movement.

Juan Posadas. An Argentine who, in 1962, led a split of ultraleft and sectarian elements from a number of Latin American sections of the Fourth International. The split had been preceded by a period of estrangement and disagreement with the majority of the Fourth International over a number of questions including the Cuban Revolution, with the Posadistas becoming more and more hostile to the Castro regime. The split-off movement created considerable confusion at first by claiming to be *the* Fourth International and so labelling their publications.

3. APRA began in Peru in 1924. Its five-point program was: action against Yankee imperialism; the unity of Latin America; industrialization and land reform; the internationalization of the Panama Canal; and world solidarity of all people and oppressed classes. APRA later degenerated into a liberal, anticommunist, procapitalist reform party, and as such it continues to play a role in Peruvian politics. It was outlawed in 1931 and again in 1948, but was legalized in 1956.

4. *Cuzco.* The name of the department in southeastern Peru and its capital city. The city of Cuzco, located in the luxuriant

valley of the Huatanay River, the original center of the great Inca empire, is today the sixth largest city in Peru. The department of Cuzco is one of the twenty-four departments into which the country is divided politically; both in area and population it is one of the largest in Peru.

5. *Prado.* Manuel Prado y Ugarteche, leader of the Partido Democratico Peruano (Democratic Peruvian Party), president of Peru from 1939 to 1947, and from 1956 to 1961.

Chapter 2

1. *Quechua.* The chief language of the ancient Incas, still the language of the Indians of the *sierra*, although with considerable local variations. Quechua is the sole language of some 30 percent of the population. Another 15 to 20 percent speak both Quechua and Spanish, the country's official language.

2. *Pedro Beltrán.* Became finance minister and premier in 1959 under President Prado; the chief figure in carrying out the Prado government's program.

3. *Manuel Gonzales Prada* (1848-1918). Peruvian poet, radical philosopher, and essayist; a left liberal; he raised the Indian question in Peruvian literature, maintaining that Peru could not really become a nation until the Indian was integrated into its society.

4. *Fernando Belaúnde Terry.* President from 1963 until his overthrow by a military junta in October 1968. Haya de La Torre, the APRA leader, had won a slim victory in the 1962 presidential elections; the military nullified the election by a coup, but allowed a new election in 1963. This was won by Belaúnde with the backing of the AP-DC coalition (Belaúnde's Popular Action Party and the Christian Democratic Party).

5. *"Revolutionary" title.* The military junta, led by General Juan Velasco Alvarado, which overthrew Belaúnde in October 1968, and rules the country today, calls itself the "Revolutionary Government."

Chapter 3

1. *APRA Rebelde.* Literally, "Rebel APRA." A left split-off, primarily of youth elements, from APRA in the early 1960s; it

was distinguished by its support of the Cuban Revolution. Later, the MIR (Movimento de Izquierda Revolucionaria — Movement of the Revolutionary Left) developed out of the APRA Rebelde elements.

Chapter 4

1. *Pierre Frank.* A leader of the Fourth International and its French section, the Ligue Communiste. The citation is from his article "The Transitional Program" in *International Socialist Review,* May-June 1967, p. 4.

Chapter 5

1. This citation from Trotsky, and all those that follow in this chapter are from pp. 206-15, Chapter XI, "Dual Power" in *The History of the Russian Revolution,* vol. 1. Reprinted with permission of the University of Michigan Press.

2. *Another falsehood.* Among others, Régis Debray has made this charge. Cf. his "Revolution in the Revolution?" *Monthly Review,* July-August 1967, p. 36ff.

Chapter 6

1. *Foco.* This Spanish word means a center of guerrilla operations, rather than a military base in the ordinary sense.

2. *Permanent revolution.* The Marxist theory elaborated by Trotsky. It states, among other things, that in order to accomplish and consolidate even bourgeois-democratic tasks such as land reform in an underdeveloped country, the revolution must go beyond the limits of a democratic revolution into a socialist revolution that sets up a workers' and peasants' government. Such a revolution therefore will not take place in "stages" (first a stage of capitalist development to be followed at some time in the future by a socialist revolution), but will be continuous or "permanent," passing immediately to a postcapitalist stage. For a full exposition of the theory, see Trotsky's *The Permanent Revolution and Results and Prospects,* 1969, Pathfinder Press, New York.

3. *Putschism.* From the German word *putsch,* a secretly planned and swiftly executed attempt to overthrow the government by force.

Chapter 7

1. *Túpac Amaru.* A descendant of the Inca rulers who led an
Indian revolt against the Spaniards and was beheaded in the
public square in Cuzco in 1571. Also an eighteenth-century
descendent of the Incas who took the name Túpac Amaru.
He led a struggle which began as a *mestizo* movement in
1780 and developed into an Indian upsurge against Spanish
colonial rule. It was suppressed in 1783 and was followed by
widespread executions and repression.

To My People

1. *José Carlos Mariátegui* (1895-1930). A Marxist writer and
organizer; founded the Socialist Party of Peru in 1928, in
opposition to APRA. In addition to his political and organizational work, Mariátegui had a great influence on literary and
cultural thought, particularly through his magazine *Amauta,*
begun in 1926 and published until 1930.

Mariátegui founded the General Confederation of Peruvian
Workers (CGTP), the first workers' organization in Peru. During his life, it was very militant, but later it was tamed by the
Stalinists. It finally disappeared and was replaced by the Confederation of Peruvian Workers (CTP) set up by the APRA.
The CTP in turn became increasingly conservative and discredited; and consequently, the CGTP has been revived, though
in a bureaucratized form. Following the Communist Party line,
the CGTP supports the present military dictatorship. Blanco
and his fellow Trotskyists work within the CGTP to make it
more democratic and its program more representative of the
workers' interests. The CTP follows the line of APRA, which is
to the right of the present military government.

2. *Gusanos.* The Spanish word for worms, popularized by the
Cubans in the 1960s as an epithet for counterrevolutionaries.

Puno: The Masses Mobilize

1. *Aliancistas.* Members or supporters of the "alliance" between
Belaúnde's Popular Action party and the Christian Democrats,
which held the executive power in the government. Control of
the Chamber of Deputies was held by the "coalition" of the
APRA and the UNO (the ultraright party of ex-dictator General
Odría).

2. *Puno.* The name of the department directly southeast of Cuzco and of the departmental capital. The town of Puno is the only large town in the vast intermontane basin (*puna*) that comprises most of the department.

3. *Cáceras family.* Politically active merchants in Puno, who controlled the Puno Departmental Union Front.

4. *Agrarian Reform.* On the pretext that the peasants were too ignorant to farm the land efficiently if they owned it, the 1964 law did not call for wholesale expropriation of the big haciendas. The government retained discretionary power to designate specific areas where land redistribution was considered desirable. Owners of any expropriated land had to be compensated in cash or bonds. The most productive and efficiently run farms, such as those on the coast producing export crops, were specifically exempted by decree from any expropriation.

5. *Popular Cooperation.* President Belaúnde's scheme for national economic development. Rather than socializing the national resources as the base for a developmental plan, his Popular Cooperation program required the peasants to take the initiative and do the work of building schools, hospitals and roads, and clearing virgin lands, etc., while the government promised to provide technical assistance. Belaúnde justified this by declaring that Peru should look back to the Inca Empire for inspiration and that each remote Andean village should work as a community to improve its conditions. This scheme put the main responsibility for national economic development on the peasants, the most poverty-stricken section of society.

Puna, a Story

1. *Puna.* The name given in the south of Peru to the region of wide, undulating plateaus between the eastern and western Cordilleras of the Andes. This *puna* or *altiplano* is a vast intermontane basin approximately 500 miles long and 100 miles wide, with a mean altitude of 12,000 feet, sloping gently to the south. It is very cold and dry. Earthquakes are frequent throughout the area.

2. *Coca.* A bush that grows in the Andean highlands and from which cocaine is derived. Its leaves are chewed by the poor

people of Peru and Bolivia; they produce a narcotic effect against the hunger, thirst, cold, heat, pain, and weariness that are the common lot of the Indians.

3. *Llika.* Spider web or caterpillar cocoon with which some coca is adulterated and which is injurious to the chewer's health.

The Teacher

1. *José María Arguedas* (1913-1969). Peruvian author of stories and novels treating Indian themes with a sober but intense lyricism. He spent his childhood in an Indian community, and Quechua was his first language; only later did he learn Spanish. Although he wrote in Spanish, he developed an original style that followed Quechua syntax and sentence construction, thus affording the reader a greater insight than ever before into the Indian mode of thought and expression. In addition to his literary accomplishments, Arguedas was noted for his investigations of Indian folklore and was head of the Institute of Ethnological Studies of the National Museum of Peru. He committed suicide in 1969.

2. *Chuño.* Potatoes preserved by the Indians by a process of drying and freezing.

3. *Tayta.* The Quechua word for father, used as a term of respect and affection to an older person.

4. *Warak'as.* Quechua word meaning sling for hurling stones, one of the principal weapons of the ancient Incas.

5. *Rangers.* Special antiguerrilla units of the Peruvian and most other Latin American armies, trained (and sometimes officered) by the U. S. military.

My Tayta José María
and the Indian Aspect of the Peruvian Revolution

1. *César Vallejo* (1892-1938). Peru's most famous poet. Identified with most of the modernist trends in poetry in the 1920s, he retained a deep interest in regional, popular, and Indian subjects. He lived in Europe from 1923 on; visited the USSR twice; joined the Communist Party in 1931; wrote political novels and plays, which were not very successful. Attended

a writers' congress in Spain in 1936, the year the Spanish Civil War broke out. He returned to Paris, already a sick man, to aid efforts to raise support for the antifascist struggle in Spain; died in 1938. His *Poemas Humanas* and poems on the Spanish Civil War were published posthumously.

Further on in this chapter, the author refers to Vallejo as a "universal *cholo*." This term *cholo* is used in Peru to denote an Indian and also a *mestizo,* a person of mixed Indian and Spanish ancestry. "When I refer to Vallejo as a 'universal *cholo*,'" Blanco writes, "I mean that at the same time he is very native, very local, and very universal, very international and very much an internationalist."

2. *Indio sonqo. Indio* is the Spanish adjective for Indian; *sonqo* is the Quechua word for heart.

3. *Huayno.* A type of song in the Peruvian highlands; plaintive and elegiac; the verses are marked by metaphor and allusions.

Quena. A reed flute.

4. *Ciro Alegría* (1909-   ). Peru's most famous novelist on Indian subjects. One of the early leaders of APRA; imprisoned 1931-33 and exiled 1934 for his pro-Indian and socialist agitation. His best known novels are *La serpiente de oro* (The Golden Serpent) published in 1935; *Los perros hambrientos* [The Hungry Dogs], 1939; and *El mundo es ancho y ajeno* (Broad and Alien Is the World), 1941. *The Golden Serpent* and *Broad and Alien Is the World* have been published in the U.S. in translations by Harriet Onís. All three novels portray the community life of the Indians in various remote regions of Peru, their struggle against the forces of nature and man's injustices.

Luis E. Valcárcel. A Peruvian anthropologist and writer.

José Sabogal. An artist who introduced the element of Indianism into modern Peruvian painting.

Alviña. Composer at the beginning of this century who wrote very elaborate music without, however, losing the Indian spirit of his compositions.

Julio C. Tello (1880-1947). Peruvian Indian scholar, whose work is internationally known in archaeological circles.

5. *Ollantay.* A verse drama in Quechua, supposedly written before the Spanish Conquest. It was discovered by a priest between 1770 and 1780. Its title is the name of the protagonist, an Indian whose presumptuous love for an Inca princess provides the play's dramatic conflict. Considered the first important example of American Indian literature.

6. *Clorinda Matto de Turner* (1854-1909). Peruvian novelist; wife of an English doctor. A pioneer of the social novel dealing with the Indians. A crusader for social reform, she is chiefly known for *Aves sin nido* (Birds Without a Nest), a novel that exposes the landowners' injustices to the Indians.

7. *Yawar Fiesta.* A novel by José María Arguedas that shows how profoundly certain cruel rites have impregnated Indian customs. *Yawar* is the Quechua word for blood.

8. *Los Ríos Profundos* (The Deep Rivers). A novel by José María Arguedas published in 1959; it relates the story of a mestizo boy raised by the Indians who is later sent to be educated in a small-town high school of a boring and gloomy atmosphere. Although it deals with poverty, injustice, and suffering, the book has an optimistic and lyrical quality.

9. *Manan.* Quechua word for a very emphatic "no" or "impossible."

Mistis. Quechua word for all non-Indians, such as whites, Blacks, mestizos.

10. *Mariátegui.* See Note 1 of *To My People* (p. 162).

11. *Quechua.* The national language of the Inca peoples, the sole language of over 30 percent of Peru's population.

Aymara. Another Indian language of the *sierra*, spoken by about 4 percent of the population, mainly in the department of Puno and around Lake Titicaca.

Guarani. Indian people and language of the lowland forests in the eastern part of Peru.

12. *Yaraví.* A type of Peruvian music and singing derived from the ceremonial music and dances for the dead of the Quechua Indians.

13. *Manuel Acosta Ojeda.* A composer of protest songs and other music. Though a creole, he composes *huaynos* and other music in indigenous forms.

Pastorita Huaracina, Jilguero Huascarán, and "La Sureñita"
Lucila Sánchez. These three singers and composers of *huaynos* and other types of native music are culturally very indigenous. They are all from the mountain districts. Much of their composition and repertory is protest music.

14. *Alicia Maguiña.* Composer and singer. She is from "creole" Peru, that is, from the coast, the part of Peru where the Indian influence is least strong. She has written a few protest songs, among them "Indio," some of whose imagery Blanco has used in the paragraph mentioning her. A nonpoetic translation of the relevant passages of "Indio" is included below:

> The light is made dark
> and the Indian is born;
> The *puna* is made human
> and the Indian is born
>
> I will hear your laugh
> and you will be joyful
> and I will be joyful.

The Earthquake: the Rich and the Poor

1. *Earthquake.* In May 1970, during the Peruvian winter, northern Peru was rocked by a tremendous earthquake. The toll was 50,000 dead and 800,000 homeless.

2. *Torreblanca.* A pun on the prefect's name, which literally means "white tower."

3. *Renrahirca.* Along with several adjacent villages, Renrahirca was devastated by an avalanche from Mt. Huascarán on January 10, 1962. Approximately 3,800 people were killed.

4. *Ancash Club.* An association of people living in Lima who originally came from Ancash, a department of Peru on the central Pacific coast.

The Government, the Oligarchy, and the Exploited

1. *Subsistence.* It is estimated that one-third of Peru's population of 12 million lives virtually outside the market economy.

2. *UNO— Union Nacional Odrista.* The party headed by General Odría, the former dictator.

3. *AP-DC Alliance.* The alliance between Belaúnde's party, *Acción Popular* [Popular Action], and *Democrata Cristiano* [Christian Democratic Party].

4. *The Page 11 Scandal.* This centered around the "disappearance" of a page of the signed agreement between the Belaúnde government and the International Petroleum Company. It was rumored to have contained a clause favorable to Peru. This scandal broke shortly before the military coup that brought the present government to power and served as an immediate pretext for that coup.

5. *The FLN.* The National Liberation Front (Frente de Liberación Nacional), an organization formed by the Peruvian Communist Party with left and liberal elements. It was set up for the 1962-63 electoral campaign and reached its high point then. Afterwards, the principal FLN figures developed differences with the CP apparatus and the latter was expelled. The FLN continued as an independent opportunist organization. When the present military junta seized power, the FLN supported it. At present it hardly exists as an organization, its former leaders all working on their own individual accounts.

Glossary of Foreign Words

achiote- seed of the annatto tree, used for making dyes

aliancistas- members of the Popular Action/Christian Democrat alliance

arriendo- plot of land belonging to the peasant, for his use

arroba- measure of weight, roughly equivalent to twenty-five pounds

ayllu- peasant commune or communal village

ayni- collective work done by peasants in the communal village

campesino- peasant

careo- court confrontation of accused by witnesses

causachu- Quechua equivalent of the Spanish *viva!*; translated in English as "long live" as in "Long live Hugo Blanco!"

chicha- strong drink, similar to beer, popular in Peru

cholo- Peruvian term used to denote both Indians and mestizos

chuño- potatoes preserved by the Indian method of drying and freezing

ch'upo- literally an infected boil or tumerous growth, here used to refer to the Soviet bureaucracy

coca- a bush that grows in the Andean highlands, from which cocaine is derived; narcotic effect produced by chewing the leaves

comunero- a member of the peasant commune or *ayllu*

compañero- Spanish word for comrade

compañerokuna- Quechua word for comrades

conquistadores- Spanish military forces who invaded, conquered, and occupied the continent of South America for the Spanish colonial empire in the sixteenth century; used especially in Mexico and Peru

faena- unpaid labor on road repair; one of the peasants' obligations to the *gamonal*

foco- base used for guerrilla operations

gamonal- at once the peasant's landlord and boss; roughly equivalent to a plantation owner

gorilla- expression meaning militarist

gringo- Spanish term for foreigner or stranger; often used disparagingly of the English or North Americans in Latin America

Guardia Civil- the state police

gusanos- Spanish word meaning worms, popularized during the Cuban Revolution as an epithet for counterrevolutionaries

hacienda- large estate or plantation belonging to a *gamonal*

huayno- type of song in the Peruvian highlands, marked by metaphors and allusions

Indio- Spanish word meaning "Indian"

kulaks- Russian expression meaning rich peasant

latifundia- great landed estates or plantations with primitive agriculture, using servile peasant labor

layqa- Indian word for witchcraft

llaqhta taytas- Quechua for "distinguished citizens"

llika- spider web or caterpillar cocoon with which some coca has been adulterated; injurious to the user's health

llunk'us- expression for "intruder" in Quechua

manan- Quechua for "absolutely no!"

mestizos- those of mixed, Spanish and Indian, ancestry

minifundia- small, sometimes miniscule farm or plot of land

misti- expression used to denote any non-Indian

mit'ani- domestic labor in the landlord's house, required of the peasant women, similar to the *pongo*

montoneros- in the nineteenth and early twentieth centuries, groups of peasants armed by *gamonales* and used in their service for internecine warfare with other *gamonales*

nabos hauch'a- stewed leaves of the mustard tree, often eaten by peasants for want of anything better

oca- a sorrel with edible tuberous roots

ojotas- Indian women's sandals

olluco- a vine with edible tuberous roots

palla- labor of peasant women and children owed to the *gamonal*

p'ata kiska- a variety of cactus

pongo- unpaid domestic labor in the *gamonal's* house; another of the peasant's obligations to the landlord

propio- unpaid peasant labor transporting produce for the *gamonal*

pujiu- Quechua word for spring

puna- grass-covered, windswept plains between the Eastern and Western cordilleras of the Andes in Peru

Qelquan riman- Quechuan idiom meaning "what is written is what is heard"

quena- a reed flute

quinoa- a pigweed whose seeds are ground up and used as cereal

selva- forrested slopes in Peru

sonqo- Quechua word for heart

tarwi- the fruit of a leguminous plant

tayta- Quechua word meaning father; used as an affectionate, respectful term for any elder

unchucha- plant with fragrant white flowers and edible roots

venceremos- first person plural of the Spanish verb *vencer,* to win; *venceremos* or "we will win" was popularized as a revolutionary slogan during the Cuban Revolution

wank'a- a kind of smooth, very hard stone

warak'a- sling for hurling stones; principal weapon of the early Incas

yaravi- type of Peruvian music and singing derived from the ceremonial music and dances for the Quechua dead

wayra- Quechua word for winter

yawar- blood; the Yawar Fiesta is an ancient Indian ritual

yerbaje- surrender of some of the peasant's livestock to the *gamonal,* another of the peasant obligations to the landlord

yunka- Quechua for "inside"; refers in this context to the transitional geographic areas called the "valleys" in Cuzco

Index

Abril, Paco 19
Acción Popular 147, 160n, 168n
Afro-Americans 30, 133
Aguilar brothers 37
Aguirre, Hernando 19
Alegría, Ciro 131, 165n
Almirón, Avelino 37
alpaca 25
Alviña 131, 165n
Amalgamated Union of Newspaper Retailers 21
Amaru, Túpac 82, 97, 122, 128, 151, 162n
Amauta (magazine) 162n
Amazon River 26, 30
American Popular Revolutionary Alliance (Alianza Popular Revolucionaria Americana — APRA) 19, 48, 61, 68, 79, 116, 121, 147, 151, 159n, 160n, 162n, 165n
Ancash Club 143, 167n
Andes mountains 25, 26, 28
Andrade, Clemente 37
Angles, Victor 77
AP-DC Alliance 101, 147, 160n, 162n, 168n
APRA (see American Popular Revolutionary Alliance)
APRA Rebelde 38, 160n
Aragón, Antonio 22, 38, 39, 86
Aranjuez 37
Arequipa 37, 77
Arguedas, José María 126, 130-34, 164n

Artola, Armando 16
Ayaviri 101, 102
ayllu 27, 28, 29, 58, 116, 127
Aymara 133, 166n
ayni 28

bank expropriations 39, 56, 66, 75, 87-89
Batista, Fulgencio 63
Battilana, Alfredo 77, 79, 81, 89
Beingolea, Lucio 37, 96
Béjar, Héctor 8, 15, 90
Belaúnde Terry, Fernando 14, 34, 84, 88, 147, 160n, 163n, 168n
Beltrán, Pedro 28, 160n
Bodero, Luis Zapata 38
Bolaños, Tiburcio 69, 80
Bolívar, Simón 27, 28
Bravo, Douglas 8

Caboy, Vega 48
Cáceres family 101, 102, 163n
Caller, Laura 77
Canal, Manuel 37
Candela, Pedro 66, 86
Candia, Carmen 136
Carazas, Humberto 37, 96
Carpio, Gerardo 37, 96
Carpio, Leonidas 37, 96, 117
Carrión, Jorge 93, 117
Casafranca, Dalmiro 48, 95
Castro, Fidel 11, 63
Cerro de Pasco Copper Corporation 51, 119, 139

CGTP (see General Confederation of Peruvian Workers)

Chalco, Marcial 77

Charmorro, Lorenzo 86, 127-30

Chaupimayo, Peasant Union of 8, 9, 21, 34, 37, 39-40, 49, 57-59, 61, 64-69, 84, 85, 86, 113, 116-18, 125, 135, 153

Cheidze, N. S. 55

Chinese Revolution 43, 56

chunchos 26, 27

Civil Guards 11, 12, 25, 51, 59, 60, 68, 69, 78, 79, 80, 90, 117, 137, 138

colonial period 27, 28, 30

Committees for the Defense of the Revolution 151

Communist Party of Cuba 43

Communist Party of Peru 14, 19, 22-23, 31, 33, 34, 37, 38, 43, 44-46, 48, 49, 50, 51, 61, 64, 65, 66, 67, 68, 69, 79, 150, 151, 152

"Communist Party (Leninist)" 38

comuneros 29

Confederation of Peruvian Peasants (Confederación de Campesinos de Peru) 21

Confederation of Peruvian Workers (Confederación de Trabajadores de Peru — CTP) 151, 162n

conquistadores 28

constitution 29

Contreras 37

cooperatives 34, 35, 115, 123-24, 157

Creus, Eduardo 13, 15, 16, 38

crops 25-27, 32

CTP (see Confederation of Peruvian Workers)

Cuba 9, 11, 43, 56, 62-64, 72-74, 140, 144, 158, 159n, 161n, 162n

Cutipa, Benito 37, 68, 156

Cuzco (city) 7, 20, 21, 22, 38, 46, 51, 77, 86, 90, 127, 142, 159-60n, 162n

Cuzco (department) 19, 20, 22, 24 (map), 25ff, 36ff, 43, 44, 48, 56-57, 67, 68, 83-84, 117, 139, 141-42, 153, 159-60

Cuzco Workers Federation (Federación de Trabajadores de Cuzco — FTC) 20-21, 38, 50, 64, 85-86

Debray, Régis 8, 161n

defense campaign 12, 80-81, 100-101

De la Puente 90

Delgado, Manuel 37

democratic centralism 42

Democratic Party of Peru (Partido Democrático Peruano) 160n

Departmental Peasants Federation of Cuzco (Federación Departmental de Campesinos de Cuzco — FDCC) 22, 59, 86

dual power 53-61

Duque, Alberto 33, 86

earthquakes 139-44, 167n

El Frontón Prison Island 14, 81, passim

ELN (see National Liberation Army)

evictions 48-49

FBI 91

FDCC (see Departmental Peasants Federation of Cuzco)

Federation of Peruvian Students (Federación Estudiantil de Peru — FEP) 93, 98-100

FEP (see Federation of Peruvian Students

FIR (see Revolutionary Left Front)

FLN (see National Liberation Front)

focos 62, 161n

Fourth International 12, 44, 150, 159n

FPCC (see Provincial Peasants Federation of La Convención)

Frank, Pierre 44, 161n

Frías, Ismael 15, 19, 150

FTC (see Cuzco Workers Federation)

Galdós, Zenón 127

Gamarra, Huarcaya 86

General Confederation of Peruvian Workers (Confederación General de Trabajadores de Peru — CGTP) 143, 151-52, 162n

Giraldo, Carmela 37

GOM (see Marxist Workers Group)

Gonzales, Andrés 21, 37, 49, 116

Guarani 133, 166n

Guardia Civil (see Civil Guards)

Guevara, Antonio 37

Guevara, Che 90

Hanqo, Claudio 38

Haya de la Torre 88, 160n

Heraud, Javier 90

Hernani, Fernando 80

History of the Russian Revolution, The 53-56, 161n

Howes, Carlos 19

Huadquiña 37

Huallpa, Justo 38

Huamán, Mario 90-91

Huamán, Remigio 69, 97

Huiro 64, 116

Incan Empire 27, 28, 160n

independence 28

Intelligence Police (PIP) 11, 90

Jiménez, Salustio 86

Kerensky, Alexander 55

kulaks 72-73n, 41

Laberrera, Blanca 40, 86

La Convención 21, 22, 25, 30, 35, 36, 37, 38, 40, 45, 46, 50, 51, 56, 57, 61, 63, 64-70, 83-84, 113, 117, 118, 119, 122, 123, 125, 144, 153, 156, 158

La Joya 37, 67

Lanado, Vicente 37, 94, 136-38

Lares 22, 25, 26, 30, 31, 35, 37, 38, 40, 51, 52, 61, 65, 66, 67, 68, 69, 86, 156, 158

La Sepa Penal Camp 142

Lauramarca 45

Law of Yanaconaje 45

Lenin, V. I. 42-43

Ley de Bases 84

Ligue Communiste 161n

Lima 15, 16, 20, 21, 22, 36, 38, 39, 50, 135, 144

llama 25

Loayza, Héctor 22, 86

López, Urbano 86

Luxemburg, Rosa 44

Lvov, Prince Georgi 55

Mándor 37

Maranura 37
Mariátegui, José Carlos 39, 133, 162n
Martorell, José 38, 39
Marxist Workers Group (Grupo Obrero Marxista — GOM) 19
Matto, Clorinda 132, 166n
mestizos 30, 131
minimum program 43, 44
MIR (see Movement of the Revolutionary Left)
mistis 46
montoneros 64, 132-33
Moreno, Nahuel 19, 75
Movement of the Revolutionary Left (Movimiento de la Izquierda Revolucionaria — MIR) 13, 38
Muñoz, Aniceto 37, 49, 86, 96

National Liberation Army (Ejército de Liberación Nacional — ELN) 51
National Liberation Front (Frente de Liberación Nacional — FLN) 150, 168n
National Pro-Odría Union (Unión Nacional Odriísta — UNO) 147, 168n
National Society of Industries 149
Neyra, Hugo 7, 93
Nixon, Richard 20

Oblitas, Luna 81
Odría, Manuel 19, 21, 88, 159n, 168n
Ollantay 132, 166n
Ongoy 58, 76, 123
Oropeza 129
Oviedo, Simón 116-18, 156

Pablo, Michel 19, 159n

Pachachaca Grande 37, 49, 86
Pacheco, Estenio 86
page eleven scandal 147, 168n
Paltaybamba 37, 61, 137
Pancorbo, Sebastián 137
Pasco 51, 58, 134
Pata-pata hacienda 127
Peasant Union of San Jerónimo 86
Pereyra, Daniel 22, 38, 39, 74, 75, 86
permanent revolution 74, 161n
Picol Hill 128
Pillpinto 30, 86, 116
Popular Cooperation 102, 121, 163n
POR (see Revolutionary Workers Party)
POR (newspaper) 20
Posadas, Juan 19, 159n
Potrero 37
Prada, Manuel Gonzales 30, 160n
Prado, Manuel 21, 28, 160n
Provincial Peasants Federation of La Convención (Federación Provincial de Campesinos de la Convención — FPCC) 21-22, 48ff, 65, 86, 156n
Pujiura 70, 77, 79
puna 25, 26, 28, 72, 85, 105, 107, 108, 109, 163n
Puno 101, 103, 163n, 166n
putschism 36, 39, 73-75, 161n

Qayara 69-70
Qolla 102
Qollpani Chico 37
Qoyo 37
Quechua Indians 7-8, 10, 25, 46-47, 130-34
Quechua language 30, 46-47, 131ff, 160n, 164n, 166n

Quellomayo 37
Quillabamba 33, 37, 46, 60, 64, 65, 67

Rangers 129, 164n
Remigio Huamán Defense Brigade 70, 117, 136, 156
Renrahirca 142, 167n
Republic (of Peru) 27, 28, 30
Republican Guard 14, 78, 79, 80
Revolutionary Left Front (Frente de la Izquierda Revolucionaria — FIR) 10, 22, 38-40, 51, 65-66, 83ff, 90, 102-103, 113, 117, 118, 122, 150-51, 155
Revolutionary Workers Party (Partido Obrero Revolucionario — POR) 19-21, 36, 38
Los Ríos Profundos 132, 166n
Romainville, Alfredo 82, 94, 116
Rosas, Ronald 86
Roy, Edmundo 139
Russian Revolution 41, 42, 43, 55-56, 62, 85

Sabogal, José 131, 165n
San Miguel 70, 71
San Pablo 37
Santa María 34, 65, 117, 144
Santa Rosa 37, 61, 94
SLATO (Latin American Secretariat of Orthodox Trotskyism) 38, 74
selva 26-27, 31, 45
Shopkeepers Union 33
sierra 26-27, 30, 31, 32, 33, 45, 166n
Silva, Julio 37
Socialist Party of Peru 19, 162n

soil cultivation 28-29
Soviet Union 41-44
Spanish Conquest 28
Stalin, Joseph 42-43
Stalinism 22-23, 41-45, 62, 84, 150
students 38, 93, 98-100, 118-20, 125, 149, 154, 155
Sukhanov, Nikolai 55

Tacera (newspaper) 81
Tacna 12, 77-82, 136
Tapia, Gorki 22, 85-86
teachers 16, 34
Tello, Julio C. 131, 165n
Torreblanca 142, 167n
Torres, Fortunato 76
transitional demands 44, 125, 153-55
transitional program 44-46
Trotsky, Leon 53-56
Trotskyism 22-23, 41-59, 62ff
Tunquimayo 37
Tupayachi, Dr. 46

Union Defense Brigades 60, 64-66, 67, 70, 124
united front 32
United States 20, 30, 133, 134, 139
UNO (see National Pro-Odría Union)
Urubamba (see Vilcanota River)

Valcárcel, Luis 131, 165n
Valer, Benigno 37
Valer, Dr. 142
Vallejo, César 130, 133, 164n
Vargas, Fortunato 37, 49, 86, 117
Velasco regime 14-17, 28, 31, 34-35, 82, 88, 118, 120, 140, 145-55, 160n

Vera 37
vicuña 25
Vietnam 56, 81, 97, 101, 134, 139
Vilcanota River 26
Voz Obrera (newspaper) 150

wastelands 30
Willcamayu (see Vilcanota River)

Yanatile River 26
Yaraví 133, 166n
Yawar Fiesta 132, 166n
yunka (the valleys) 26

Zamalloa, Juvenal 85
Zapata, Lucho 51, 97
Zevallos, Félix 19